WHAT'S YOUR PROBLEM?

Become a Better B2B Marketer
by Enhancing Your Problem-Solving Skills

STEVE GOLDHABER

International Standard Book Number: 9781079683240
Library of Congress Control Number: 20-19909311

Dedication

Every day, you make choices that affect yourself and the people around you. These choices define your character. They reveal who you are and who you want to be.

Are you the type of person who takes the easy path? Have you adopted the longtime methods and assumptions of your company? Of course not.

You ask the hard questions, uncover hidden truths, and forge ahead when times are tough. It's not easy to take the more difficult path, but it's usually the right choice.

Finding and solving real business problems isn't easy. You face resistance, dead ends, and other adversity. You might doubt yourself and consider giving up. But you don't. Why not?

Because you know there's great satisfaction in solving problems, which requires curiosity, imagination, and drive. Not everyone has what it takes, but you do, and that's what makes you special.

That's why this book is dedicated to you.

Contents

Part IV

Grounding Everything in a Business Problem

Part V

Content Planning

Part VI

Content Execution

Preface

Why did I write this book? Surely there are several books about content marketing. This book is different, however, because it doesn't jump right into the "how" of content marketing. Instead, it starts with how to understand the core business problems content marketing can solve. Why is this important? Many people fail because they start with tactics. For the most impact from content marketing, you must start by defining the problem. I'll help you define the problem and understand where content marketing can add the most value. By taking this approach, you won't find yourself wasting time responding to one-off tactical requests that aren't valuable to your company.

The second reason I wrote this book is because creating content is hard. On the surface, it seems simple. You just need a writer and a designer, right? That's just one part, albeit an important part, and even that part can be challenging without the right approach. But content marketing is about much more than creating content. You need to understand the challenges facing your audience as well as how to distribute, measure, and optimize the content. This book will help you understand how to do it right.

I've been in marketing for more than twenty years. I've seen companies' content marketing, and not coincidentally the companies themselves, fail. When they fail, it's not pretty—employees, owners, and vendors struggle and experience a lot of stress. I've been there, so think of me as someone who knows what you could be facing. I've also seen companies do amazing things and flourish impressively while using content marketing. That's when it's really exciting! When done right, content marketing is incredibly powerful.

After reading this book, you'll understand the techniques for building an effective content program. You'll be able to answer real business questions, like "Did we sell more as a result of putting this program in place?" and "Do people better understand what our company does?" and "Were we able to increase customer retention?"

For this book, I've interviewed dozens of marketing experts, ranging from CMOs of Fortune 500 companies to owners of technology startups to longtime content marketing professionals. I'm excited to share their wisdom, along with what I've learned during my career, and to help you advance your own career. Content marketing can seem too scary and overwhelming to tackle. But the right knowledge, which I've aimed to provide here, is a powerful tool.

Acknowledgments

It takes a lot to write a book. The author's effort can be successful only if everyone around him or her helps to make it happen.

First and foremost, I thank my wife, Carolyn, who put up with me getting up at 4:30 every morning. She consistently delivered the morning line, "Why are you up so early? . . . Oh yeah, the book," with a combination of support and eye rolling.

To Charlie, our six-year-old, who often joined me in my office at that hour. He reminded me that some things in life are out of my control, taught me to be flexible, and demonstrated the power of a smile to get what one wants. Like homemade waffles at 5 a.m.

To Andrew, our nine-year-old, who taught me that life doesn't have to be complex. Sometimes you just have to find what brings you happiness. Like playing soccer and baseball for many uninterrupted hours.

Thanks go to my father, Richard, who has written several books of his own—fourteen to be exact. He taught me that life requires hard work; there are no shortcuts.

And to my mom, Jeanne, who is most likely shopping now. She taught me the power of asking for what you want—the worst that could happen is that you're told no.

In addition, many people who helped shaped my career. I was fortunate that my first job after college was at U.S. Satellite Broadcasting (now DirecTV and owned by AT&T). At the time, I couldn't foresee how the customer-centric culture that the Hubbard family created there would have such a significant impact on my career.

In addition, I would like to acknowledge the following people for helping me shape the ideas in this book. Whether our conversations were brief or took hours, without their time and generosity, this book wouldn't be filled with different perspectives and various examples. Thank you to Michelle Adams, Josh Anisfield, Arti Arora, Tim Blair, Ed Bourelly, Sean Callahan, Tony Christos, Winn Clark, Phil Clement, Regis Coccia, Marcos Colón, Chris Carollo, Al Czervik, Tony D'Annunzio, Andy Dufresne, Howard Eirinberg, Camille Fetter, David Fisher, Andy Foote, Ross Freedman, Bill Furlong, Penny Gillhaus, Russell Glass, Greg Green, Sue Hardek, Tari Haro, Nick Hartman, Sean Hazen, Eliot Hart-Nelson, Scott Hays, Jennifer Hodroge, Courtney Hyde, Samantha Isdale, Daniel James, Bonni Kaplan, Bob Katula, Sara Kennedy, Andrea Kroll, Glenn LaFolette, Chris Lawson, Venetta Linas Paris, Maggie Lower, Paulo Martins, Corby Marx, Rob McGillen, Joslyn McIntyre, Pam McNamara, Andrew Miller, Laurel Miltner, Tom O'Connell, Akash Pathak, Nora Peterson, Alex Prosperi, David Prosperi, Claire Keys Pytlik, Iman Rahim, Scott Rhodes, Manny Rivera, Heather Ronnow, Patrick Rooney, Cybil Rose, Lee Rosenthal, Eric Sawitoski, Anne Schmitt, Matt Scroggins, Ajit Sivadasan, Jackie Stone, Clay Stelzer, Anamaria Stefan, John Stewart, Lacey Underall, Jenny Uyeda, James Warda, Keith Wiegold, Katherine Willhoite, Kathleen Wolf, and Jacques Zimmerman.

I've done my best to identify the sources of quotations and concepts discussed here. Any errors or omissions are my own.

Introduction

I've worked in marketing for more than twenty years. I started at the bottom of the food chain, as an intern, in 1996. After a handful of job changes and promotions, on both the client and the agency side, I eventually worked my way up to being an executive vice president at a Fortune 500 company.

Along the way, I worked with some amazing people and companies. For the record, I've also worked with a handful of mediocre companies, and not-so-amazing people. I'm grateful for both the good and bad experiences, which were equally important to my professional growth.

A theme that has run through my career is helping people understand the power of digital marketing. I've always loved helping people understand how to use the channel effectively. Many of these conversations started with tactical requests, like "I need a website, an app, and an infographic! Can you build them for me?"

While I loved people's passion, these requests weren't grounded in anything strategic. They were just "cool" things they wanted, or their boss' wanted. To help people understand what they actually needed, I always asked them the same question: "What's your problem?"

This question forced people to think strategically about the problem they needed to solve. When I asked the question, most people didn't have an answer. Eventually, after they uncovered the answer, our conversations were more focused and productive.

Asking "What's your problem?" continued to guide me, and the people I've worked with, over the years. I believed in the power of this question so much that I decided to write a book about it. Yes, the book you're reading now.

Content marketing has gained traction in the business-to-business (B2B) space in the past five to nine years. Brands wanted to become publishers. Suddenly, journalists' skills were in demand again, this time from businesses hoping to increase their sales by improving their marketing.

Companies wanted their own publishing platforms, and they sought great writers who knew a specific industry. It was like another gold rush.

Content marketing is far from new, however. It actually has been around for a while.

Are you familiar with the Michelin Guide to fine dining? Of course you are. More than a century old, it is the standard for evaluating restaurants. Chefs and restaurant owners do everything they can to earn a one-, two-, or three-star rating. I've been fortunate to eat at several Michelin-rated restaurants, always a memorable experience (in a good way).

How do restaurants request a Michelin rating? They don't. There's no application fee, and Michelin decides which restaurants its critics will visit and which select few will be rated and included in the guide. That policy, combined with the high standards and anonymity of its critics—as well as the guide's clear, consistent, and accurate contents—makes it a credible source of helpful information.

Why bring up restaurant ratings in a book about content marketing? The Michelin guide is an early example of great content marketing. Although at the time there were only three thousand cars in France, brothers André and Édouard Michelins started up the guide in 1889 with the goal of selling tires.[1] How does one sell more tires? Sell more cars. Why would anyone need a car in France in the late 1800s? To explore the countryside, of course, staying at nice hotels and enjoying wonderful dining.

The brothers created a free book of useful information for the traveler—including maps and hotel and dining information. They could have called it "*Look at All the Amazing Experiences You Can Have If Only You Had a Car!*" The brothers hoped that, once the idea had been implanted, people's next thought would be, "Hey, maybe it's time to buy a car."

This is the spirit of content marketing: Move your audience closer to a business goal—whether it's identifying potential purchasers of a product or service, increasing customer engagement, or boosting sales—by providing people with content they find useful.

You see, traditionally, most marketing has consisted of company-centric messages. It's been about telling prospective customers that your company has an interesting product or service available for purchase. Content marketing is different; it's about using content to build trust first, before anything is

---

[1]Martin Chalakoski, "Michelin Red Guide: How a Tire Company Became the Taste Maker for the World's Best Restaurants," *The Vintage News*, December 29, 2015, https://www.thevintagenews.com/2015/12/29/43088/.

bought or sold. How do you build trust? By genuinely helping people in a way that doesn't benefit the company . . . at least not initially. It's about changing the nature of the customer dynamic. It's about making people feel as if they're buying from a company, not being sold to.

Although not new, as the Michelin Guide example shows, content marketing is flourishing more than ever today, especially at B2B companies. Why? In today's marketplace, the way information is delivered to consumers has changed, generally from a broadcast to an on-demand consumption model, which allows people to avoid ads more easily. Sure, advertising still exists, and it can work, but its effectiveness isn't what it was. In addition, companies are competing for the attention of people who, after decades of exposure to advertising, have learned to tune it out. For example, when a commercial is on TV, what's in your hand? That's right, your phone. And would you rather look at your phone or watch a commercial?

Why has content marketing become so effective, especially in the B2B world? Unlike advertising, content marketing done right isn't viewed as a nuisance. Instead, because the content is perceived as helpful, the recipient is 100 percent focused while consuming it. Companies that use content marketing have a better chance of selling more. After all, developing customer relationships in the B2B world is all about trust. If your company can use content to help build that trust, it has an advantage over its competitors.

Consider the customer's perspective as well. Would you rather be sold something or make the decision to buy something? The spirit of content marketing is that the customer is being helped to make the best purchase; he or she doesn't feel sold to. This may appear to be mere semantics, but it's a very important distinction. Why? When you're buying something, it's fun. And you, not a salesperson or a marketer, are in control of the experience.

By the way, the Michelin Guide is now priced from $19 to $25, and according to its website, "rates over 30,000 establishments in over 30 territories across three continents, and more than 30 million Michelin Guides have been sold worldwide." The book is no longer a piece of content marketing; now, the guide is itself the product.

part I

WHY GREAT CONTENT MARKETING STARTS WITH IDENTIFYING A PROBLEM

Many content marketers are excited by the idea of creating content and jump right in with both feet. Their enthusiasm is misguided, however, if they haven't first determined the real problem their efforts need to solve. This section demonstrates why starting with the problem is the key to effective content marketing.

CHAPTER 1

Why Should B2B Companies Use Content Marketing?

Gloucester is located on Cape Ann in Essex County, Massachusetts. With a population of about 30,000, the town is known for commercial fishing, which is incredibly physical and dangerous work.

In 1991, Captain Frank Payne Jr. and five crew members encountered an unusual storm. Their fishing ship, the *Andrea Gail*, battled hurricane-force winds and waves up to 100 feet high. No one aboard survived the powerful storm. According to Bob Case, who spent more than thirty years as a meteorologist in New England, this storm was so intense because of "an unprecedented set of circumstances." First, a high pressure system from Canada provided a large pool of cold air. At the same time, there was a low-pressure system of warm air in the area. Finally, a dying hurricane Grace, which had moved north after forming south of Bermuda, provided "immeasurable tropical energy."[2] These three meteorological events converged in the same place at the same time to create what author Sebastian Junger later named his book, "the perfect storm."

What does the *Andrea Gail* story have to do with content

---

[2]Servpro of Cambridge/Belmont blog, "NOAA Meteorologist Bob Case, the Man Who Names the Perfect Storm," June 16, 2000, https://www.servprocambridgebelmont.com/blog/post/50389/storm/noaa-meteorologist-bob-case-the-man-who-named-the-perfect-storm.

marketing? An unprecedented set of multiple forces is at work today in B2B marketing, creating its own perfect storm. These forces are strong, and, no matter how hard you try, you won't beat them. That is, not if you use traditional approaches to marketing.

The biggest force in B2B marketing's perfect storm is, of course, the internet. Access to information is unprecedented. This phenomenon puts B2B companies at a big disadvantage, because they are no longer the gatekeepers of the information their customers receive. The internet has created, and encouraged, on-demand direct consumption of information. We take quick and easy access to information for granted, and we've become conditioned to rely on Google for answers. Would you be surprised if I told you that more than 400 billion searches were made globally in 2008?[3] In 2012, it was up to 1.2 *trillion*. And in 2018, the number was more than two trillion.[4] It's really hard to get your head around these numbers and their rate of growth.

Another factor in marketing's perfect storm is that *buyers don't want to work with salespeople*. Why not? They don't trust them. According to Forrester, 68 percent of B2B buyers prefer to research potential purchases on their own. And 60 percent would rather not use salespeople as their primary information source.[5] Think about that for a second. More than two-thirds of the prospects you want to connect with don't want to talk to you! Think of it as revenge for all these years when salespeople were the sole gatekeepers of information about products and services.

---

[3] "How Many Hits Does Google Get a Day?," Magnetoz blog, May 12, 2016, http://www.magnetoz.com/digital-marketing/how-many-hits-does-google-get-a-day; and Search Engine Land, https://searchengineland.com/.
[4] Aleksandra, "63 Fascinating Google Search Statistics," SEO Tribunal blog, September 26, 2018, https://seotribunal.com/blog/google-stats-and-facts/.
[5] April Henderson and Laura Ramos, "Beyond The Lead: How Content Marketing Builds Lasting Relationships," Forrester Research, Inc., 2018 webinar, https://mktg.forrester.com/2018-content-marketing.

HubSpot did some research on who Americans trust.[6] Here are the percentages of respondents who consider the following people trustworthy: lobbyist (1 percent); car salesperson (1 percent);politician (1 percent); stockbroker (2 percent); salesperson (3 percent); and then, you guessed it, marketer (also 3 percent). That's even lower than I thought it would be.

Don't be tempted to put a marketing spin on these results by saying something like, "Hey, we're seen as three times more trustworthy than lobbyists, politicians, and people selling cars." Accept the sobering facts, which reinforce the idea that marketers have worked themselves into a horrible reputation.

What else has created this perfect storm? The pace of business today, which is incredibly fast. Ten years ago, people had the patience to wait two to three months to launch a general marketing program. Today, it's two or three weeks. How did this happen? Why does everything need to happen now? First, since we live in a digital world, everything is built for speed and instant gratification. Second, whatever its industry, a company probably has more competitors than it did ten years ago, and the companies that can provide buyers with quality information faster than the others have an advantage.

Yet another changing dynamic is that large companies no longer have all the advantages. For years, large, established companies dominated their markets. In the past ten years, however, smaller firms have been successful at creating comparable, often even better, offerings. How is that possible? Smaller companies can be more specialized. They don't rely on legacy IT systems. And they're probably trying harder and can move more quickly, while the large companies are stuck in meetings or working on internal presentations that don't directly benefit their customers.

[6]HubSpot Global Jobs Poll Q2 2016, of 928 global respondents, https://www.slideshare.net/HubSpot/the-hard-truth-about-marketing.

That's what your B2B company is up against. The internet controls most of the information. Your buyers don't want to be sold to. If your company doesn't respond to a prospective customer quickly, your competition will. And being big is no longer an advantage. Fun times, right?

So how do you survive, even thrive, in this perfect storm? The answer, of course, lies is content marketing.

CHAPTER 2

Why Creating a "Content Strategy" Usually Leads to Failure

In beige conference rooms all over North America, the following event occurs every day. It starts when an executive asks, "What's our content strategy?" Another senior person responds as if she's found the fountain of youth: "Wow, that's a great question. . . . You're right, we don't have a content strategy. And we need one!"

Why is this question raised so often during senior-level meetings? First, it makes the inquirer look smart—even non-markter have heard of content marketing these days, even if they're not sure what it is. Second, it might prevent the questioner from being asked some tough questions during this meeting. Third, whatever problem was being discussed has now become a marketing problem, and dealing with it has been pushed off probably onto the marketing or digital team.

The problem with this sort of content strategy discussion is that it lacks the context of the organization's business objectives and overall marketing strategy. "Content" is just a bunch of tactics; there's nothing strategic about it. Sure, you might get some traction in the short term. But, eventually, you'll wonder if any of the tactics really worked.

At my content marketing company, 26 Characters, we've stopped using the term "content strategy," replacing it with "content planning." Why? People expect a "content strategy" to be a solution for all the different sales and marketing challenges the organization is up against, from declining sales to a dysfunctional website to a tarnished corporate image. Because people seem to think there's something magical about a strategy in general and a content strategy in particular, later on they can only be disappointed. Full disclosure: I've authored several of these magical so-called strategies in the past, so I'm speaking as a reformed criminal.

What's the best way to start your content marketing journey? Don't start with a list of tactics, and don't start with a grand plan. Instead, start with the business problem that your content marketing effort is aiming to solve. I go into more detail in later chapters, but broadly speaking, the journey consists of three phases:

1. *Define the business problem or problems to be solved.*
2. *Turn that problem, or those problems, into questions.*
3. *Answer the questions.*

I know, it seems like an absurdly simple three-step effort. But it works. Why? The simple act of turning the business problem into a question illuminates what you're trying to accomplish and how to go about it. Formulating the question makes you think, "Is this the right question to be asking?"

Remember what Albert Einstein said about the power of questions? "If I had an hour to solve a problem and my life depended on the solution, I would spend the first fifty-five minutes determining the proper question to ask, for once I know the proper question, I could solve the problem in less than five minutes."

Coming up with the right questions is the hard part, but,

once the right questions have been formulated, everything else gets easier.

This problem/question approach has many advantages. First, it focuses and engages the content-marketing team. Second, you're aligned with the decision maker from the very beginning of the content-marketing journey. Third, the act of asking a question is provoking; asking questions invites exploration. Questions force people to think over and over again about potential responses to the problem to be solved, whittling down the options and refining the possible solution until the questioner can say, "Yes, I've found the best answer."

First, ask open-ended questions. Asking open-ended questions encourages critical thinking. This technique is evident all around us. For example, ever notice that when you open Twitter it says "What's happening?" The same goes for Facebook, which uses "What's on your mind?" Once the brain sees an open-ended question, it requires an exertion of energy to fill in the missing information. The mind is engaged. Thinking is stimulated. That's the beauty of asking open-ended questions.

Second, make sure a metric is associated with each question. Be sure the question is connected to a clear business objective and that a *metric* is associated with the question—that is, how to measure the answer needs to be clear, because that's how to know whether a marketing effort has been successful. How can we increase retention among current customers (measured by churn)? How many people are familiar with what our business does (measured by awareness)? How can we provide a better customer experience (measured by net promoter scores)?

So the next time you hear "What's our content strategy?," ask the questioner to define the business problem first. Turn that problem into a question. Then solve it.

CHAPTER 3

Crafting Your Content Vision to Get Alignment

Over the course of my career, I've held positions in both corporate marketing departments and advertising agencies. Among the jobs I am especially proud of was being in charge of global digital marketing and content at two different Fortune 500 companies.

These were fun jobs. I worked with people around the world, helping them use digital channels to tell stories and launch products. One day, I would find myself working on something that was brand-related. The next day, we were building an app for conference attendees. This variety made the jobs exciting and gave me a solid understanding of the different functions of the companies.

At most larger companies, many different marketing efforts by different teams are usually going on at once. This is why it's extremely important to know why any particular content marketing program is being started. If a compelling content vision isn't created upfront, the program will lack the clarity it needs to be successful.

What's the best way to start? Craft a content vision statement.

The content vision statement is typically three to five

sentences describing what the content marketing is going to be used for. The statement usually answers these five questions:

1. Why are we using content marketing in this marketing program?
2. What is the business problem we need this program to solve?
3. What audience are we talking to with this program?
4. What is this program *not* going to do?
5. What happens once this program is successful?

The answers to all these questions are extremely important. Why? An ill-defined content marketing effort will be ineffective, and, if leadership doesn't understand and agree with you about its goals, you'll end up creating a program, and content, that lacks purpose and is probably a wasted effort.

What happens if you don't write one of these vision statements? For the first couple of months, nothing; you'll be fine without one for a while. But several months later, you'll find that all those involved in creating the program, as well as its stakeholders, have crafted, at least mentally, their own vision statements. As a result, you will end up spending your days tweaking, perhaps even dismantling, the visions of other people. Can you tell I've been in this situation before? Trust me: Craft a vision statement *before* you start creating content.

I've seen five different types of visions, and therefore vision statements, for content marketing. Determining which one to adopt will provide clarity about the type of content you will publish. You need to understand all of the approaches and use the most appropriate one for the particular business problem you're trying to solve.

1. Brand-centric vision

Brand-centric content marketing usually has a high-level purpose, most often the creation of greater brand awareness. The content focuses on creating a new brand, or supporting an existing one, through emotional storytelling that demonstrates the company's positive impact. If your company has a tag-line, the content probably brings it to life. Branding, communications, and public relations departments tend to use this approach the most.

Example of a Brand-centric Vision Statement

> Our business serves a higher purpose, one beyond helping customers with our company's solutions. We use content marketing to bring the stories of people (our customers and/or our employees) to life and demonstrate our impact. This content isn't about hitting a quarterly sales number; rather, it's about building a human connection with our customers. We want to show the outside world that our company can make a difference.

John Deere creates brand-centric content and publishes it in its magazine, *The Furrow.* According to publication manager David Jones, Charles Deere, the second son of company founder John Deere, started the magazine in 1895. Jones told a conference audience in 2018, "Charles recognized that there was potential promotional value in providing an accurate, unbiased source of information to farmers at the time."[7]

The Furrow is all about farm life. For example, what challenges do one's fellow farmers face? What new technology is available? What's the best way to manage soil? These topics don't relate to farm equipment, Deere's product, but they are

[7]Mindy Smiley, "John Deere, the 'OG Content Marketer,' on How Its 123-Year-Old Magazine Endures," The Drum, May 24, 2018, www.thedrum.com/news/2018/05/24/john-deere-the-og-content-marketer-how-its-123-year-old-magazine-endures.

of interest to Deere's customers and potential customers. John Deere wants readers to think, "Deere gets it. They understand who I am."

Deere has also moved into podcasting, a perfect medium for reaching an audience at work on a farm. One episode, called "Out of the Darkness," focused on the mental health of farmers. Field editor Steve Werblow discussed with Dr. Robert Fetsch the ways farmers can identify depression and have often-difficult conversations about the condition. This podcast episode has probably saved lives, literally. What a great example of content that shows that Deere is a brand that cares about its community.

None of the content of the magazine and podcast feature John Deere products, because even a whiff of self-promotion would taint the customer trust the company has built up over the years. Jones said, "We do not talk about ourselves in the editorial space of the magazine. We take believability very seriously. We know that a reputation that has taken 175 years to build up would take only a fraction of that time to tear down."[8]

2. Helpful-friend vision

Looking to build trust a bit faster? The "helpful friend" approach might be a good option for you. As with the brand-centric approach, the content has nothing to do with the brand or products being marketed. It's all about creating content that demonstrates that the company wants to solve the customers' problems.

When deciding what to publish, ask yourself: What can

[8]Mindy Smiley, "John Deere, the 'OG Content Marketer,' on How Its 123-Year-Old Magazine Endures," The Drum, May 24, 2018, www.thedrum.com/news/2018/05/24/john-deere-the-og-content-marketer-how-its-123-year-old-magazine-endures.

our company provide customers that isn't available elsewhere? How can our company solve something that's a common issue in their industry—in other words, fix something in the world of the customer that's broken?

The goal is to get the audience to think, "Wow, this company really understands what I'm up against, and they created something that helps to solve my problem." Once you have demonstrated your company's helpfulness and goodwill through your content, the customer will be more receptive to your agenda. There are no short-term business benefits when using this approach, a factor that can impede buy-in from the powers that be. But the goodwill that this approach engenders can be incredibly helpful in the long run.

Example of a Helpful-Friend Vision Statement

We're creating this content exclusively to build trust and goodwill with our customers. We do this by demonstrating that we want to help them with [INSERT CUSTOMER PROBLEM HERE]. Once we've earned their trust, they'll be more open to having a conversation with our company. We're not using content to explain the details of why they should work with us—that comes later. This is about genuinely understanding their problems and being viewed as the company that will be able to help them solve those problems (without mentioning our products and services).

HubSpot, a SaaS solution for midsize companies, is really good at helpful-friend content marketing. It works with advertising agencies that influence software purchases. To get in front of these influencers, HubSpot decided to create helpful content just for the agencies. Rather than repurpose their existing marketing content, spinning it to be more agency friendly, HubSpot created brand-new content with titles like "Why Your Agency's Culture Matters," "How 12 Big Brands Choose Their Marketing Agency," and "The Guide to Marketing Your Agency."

Not one of these pieces discusses what HubSpot does or how HubSpot could help the customer. Of course, the content includes contact information for HubSpot. And, as long as the customer considers HubSpot content valuable, he or she is usually willing to provide, at a minimum, an email address in exchange for access to HubSpot's gated content—which allows the company to get the most from its content marketing efforts. (See Chapter 23," Content Types," for more on gated content, including when and when not to gate.)

3. Sales-journey vision

Every salesperson faces two problems. First, getting an initial meeting with a prospect. Second, having something to say when staying in touch with the customer during the often-lengthy period between meetings and when the deal is closed.

The sales-journey approach to content marketing provides content that accelerates and increases customer conversion. The goal is to reduce friction and make it easier for the prospect to say yes. The content marketer starts by getting inside the prospect's mind. What information does he or she need? How can you reduce the risk the prospect thinks he or she would be taking by agreeing to a meeting with a salesperson from your company? What facts does the prospect need before saying yes to another meeting? Would sharing testimonials from current customers be helpful? These are the types of questions you need to answer in order to take the sales-journey approach.

To determine the topics and formats of the content, start by drawing a timeline. On the left is the starting point. On the right is the finish line. Map out what prospective customers are likely to be thinking during each phase of the journey.

Then ask yourself what content they will need at each phase. At the beginning of the timeline, the content is about demonstrating your company's understanding of the prospect's industry, and perhaps includes an overview of your company. Moving along the timeline, the content might include customer testimonials, case studies, or even a customized proposal. The best part about this approach is that it can be highly customized, based on what is learned about the prospect during the journey. For example, the salesperson could send the prospect an article on a topic the prospect mentioned during a meeting.

The key is to refine your content over time, based on the customer's journey, as patterns emerge that indicate the type and frequency of content that is working. Working thoughtfully with the salesperson, the content marketer can test multiple paths for a prospect and pursue the one that proves to be most successful. Companies that commit to experimenting with new content marketing techniques will continue to improve and are likely to close more sales over time.

Example of a Sales-Journey Vision Statement

We know what it takes to close a sale and need content to advance the customer relationship. We're using content to demonstrate our expertise, better explain what we do, and show examples of how we've helped other companies. After our potential customer sees our content, he or she will be more likely to agree to meet with us and, ultimately, buy from us.

4. Customer-retention vision

The customer-retention approach to content marketing also uses a timeline but one that starts where the sales journey ends. It's about asking, "What content can maximize customer-retention?" For example: What combination of messages would-help to retain customers? Or how far out should communication about a customer's approaching contract renewal begin?

As with the customer-journey approach, you won't need to treat all customers the same way. Based on what you know about each customer, you can create multiple scenarios. For example, a group comprising unhappy customers might receive more personalized outreach and more in-person visits. Very satisfied customers might receive messages that reinforce the positive attributes of the brand. You may even ask a happy customer to provide a testimonial.

The number of scenarios can differ based on what is needed to retain a customer. The content marketer might factor in considerations such as a particular client's financial status, the client's satisfaction with the assigned account manager, or the likelihood of a competitor trying to steal the client from your company. To find out what's on the client's mind, you might send the customer a survey or set up a lunch with a subject-matter expert from your company.

Example of a Customer-Retention Vision Statement

We have already established relationships with current customers; now we need to gauge how things are going. Is our company delivering great work? Are there shortcomings we don't see? What should we know today so that we can make changes before it's too late? How can we do a good job at retaining this customer?

Having the right tools in place is critical to understanding client engagement, an indication of the likelihood of a client's retention. If done the right way, with customer-retention marketing, the company will learn a lot about its customers.

For example, I recently worked with a Fortune 500 B2B company that used content marketing not only to speak to its customers but also to understand what their engagement looked like. Why was that important? The company discovered a correlation between clients' content consumption and their likelihood to renew their contracts—an important and useful lesson. The company could then understand which accounts were at risk, and they found out months before any renewal decisions were being made. The sales team could then use these insights to develop a specific plan for each customer.

5. Product-centric vision

The traditional way to launch a product has three steps: (1) put out a press release, (2) hold an event at a trade show, and then (3) unleash the sales team. Unfortunately, it's not that easy today.

Why not? Companies launch new, or tweaked, products and services daily—making it difficult or impossible for either the press or customers to keep up. In addition, people consume media in a different way—for example, they don't rely on industry publications the way they used to. According to Statista, overall magazine ad revenues have declined rapidly, from $13.87 billion in 2010 to a projected $4.83 billion in 2021.[9] Although being mentioned in the press, whether industry publications or

[9] Sean Callahan, "The State of the Media for B2B Marketers," LinkedIn Marketing Solutions blog, July 22, 2018, using 2016 Statista data, https://business.linkedin.com/marketing-solutions/blog/b2b-beat/2018/the-state-of-media-for-b2b-marketers.

the general news media, is usually still a good thing for a company, it just doesn't have the same impact as in the past.

This is a big reason why many B2B companies have turned to content marketing. They realize that a launch doesn't happen in one big day; it can occur over several months. Many companies use the terms "soft launch" and "hard launch" to reinforce the idea that everything doesn't happen on a particular day or two. Similarly, it's common for software companies to launch a beta version of a product before rolling out a version that's closer to final.

Example of a Product-centric Vision Statement

We need people to understand the problem before we announce the solution. We use product content marketing to make sure that prospects are aware of why we created this product in the first place. Once they understand, we've earned the right to go into more detail about how the product works. But we're not going to tell the story from our perspective. We're going to capture the stories of people who have used the product so that prospects can understand the potential real impact in the marketplace.

These five common approaches to creating a content vision constitute a powerful tool at your disposal. Use them to attain alignment within your organization.

I can't emphasize enough the importance of getting alignment on your content vision. The people you need to buy into your vision are likely to nod their heads when you show them the vision statement you have crafted. Don't settle for that, though. Make sure they have focused on it, are completely on board with it, and have signed off on it. Without such an effort on your part, when it comes time to show them the actual content, they may not recall the context within which they agreed to the vision statement.

I usually get a little dramatic when seeking a stakeholder's buy-in to a content vision statement by spelling out the consequences if he or she doesn't focus on it now. I say things like, "It's really important we're all aligned; otherwise, the company will be throwing away weeks and months of work on content." I might add, "I'm not asking you to sign off on the vision today—I realize it's a big decision. Think about it for a couple days, and then let's regroup."

Another technique for getting buy-in from stakeholders is showing them the five different approaches to crafting your content vision—with four vision statements crossed out and the one that you're using circled.

These tips might seem a little silly, but, trust me, they will help you to get the alignment you need to reduce the chances of doing a lot of wasted work and experiencing frustration down the road.

part II

THE ART OF PROBLEM SOLVING

This section is about how to become a better problem solver. It details the steps in the problem-solving process and then discusses the best practices for and common barriers to solving problems.

CHAPTER 4

Introduction to Problem Solving

Mark Hyman, M.D., is a *New York Times* best-selling author and leads the Cleveland Clinic Center for Functional Medicine. Functional medicine is a form of alternative medicine that looks at all parts of the body, not just a single organ. For example, a patient with three different symptoms who receives medication treating each of those symptoms could still be sick. By diving more deeply than the symptoms, functional medicine aims to find and treat the underlying causes.

Hyman believes that the approach of most doctors is antiquated. "The way conventional medicine is practiced today is like taking the batteries out of a smoke detector instead of trying to find the fire," he said in his blog. "[It's] like trying to fix a car by listening to the noises it makes instead of looking under the hood." He also said, "I am always interested in *all* of someone's symptoms, because they are the clues to deeper imbalances. Once you find and correct those deeper imbalances, the symptoms go away."[10]

In his blog, Hyman cited a patient of his, Joe, as an example. At age forty-two, Joe took four different psychiatric

---

[10]Mark Hyman, M.D., "Why Treating Your Symptoms Is a Recipe for Disaster," https://drhyman.com/.

medications as well as medication for asthma, psoriasis, acid reflux, irritable bowel syndrome, and chronic postnasal drip. Joe was about twenty-five pounds overweight and drank three cups of coffee, several diet colas, and two glasses of wine a day. He slept for only about five or six hours a night. Using blood tests, Hyman found that Joe had inflammation, a parasite, and yeast overgrowth in his intestinal tract. He had high triglyceride levels, high blood sugar, high cholesterol, and a fatty liver as well as genetic imbalances that increased his need for vitamin B-12 and folate. His levels of vitamin D, chromium, and omega-3 fats were low.

In addition to using short-term medication to get rid of the parasite, Hyman treated Joe by addressing the root cause of Joe's symptoms, his diet. Joe eliminated refined carbohydrates and sugars as well as the gluten and dairy that were triggering inflammation in his gut. Joe cut back on coffee, stopped drinking alcohol, and started taking a daily multivitamin, fish oil, and probiotics.

According to Hyman, after three months, "Joe had lost twenty-five pounds, his triglycerides dropped from 597 to 80, and his cholesterol from 275 to 198. His folate and B12 were back to normal. His fasting blood sugar dropped from 101 to 84, which is normal, and his insulin levels dropped back to normal. And . . . his fatty liver had healed."

Why tell a medical story in a book about content marketing? Most people solve problems using the same flawed technique the medical establishment uses: they start by finding and treating the symptoms of the problems. Even though marketers have good intentions, they usually don't get to the underlying problem of what's wrong with their business. For example, your problem isn't that sales are down; it's that people don't trust your product. Although management may be tempted to address the symptom of declining sales by establishing a mandate to "sell more," increasing customers' trust in the product is what will lead to more sales.

Another medical example, this one personal, demonstrates the value of solving the problem rather than addressing the symptoms. When training for a marathon, I started to have pain in my right knee. My doctor quickly determined I didn't have a knee problem; instead, it was a problem with my right iliotibial (IT) band, the ligament that runs from the hip to the knee. When strained by running, the IT band pulls on the kneecap and causes knee pain. Stretching out the IT band before and after running took the pain away. Problem solved. Rather than telling me to take some ibuprofen, which would have reduced the pain only temporarily, my doctor understood and treated the real problem.

Most content marketing books jump right into the practice of content marketing, but doing this will get you into trouble. Content marketing is just another tactic in the marketing arsenal. Yes, content marketing tools can be sexy—who doesn't like a good infographic or a compelling video? But without a fundamental understanding of the underlying business problem, you will be unable to select the right tools.

Remember the saying "If all you have is a hammer, everything looks like a nail"? Don't be caught holding a hammer with no nail in sight. Bear in mind that content marketing won't solve every business problem. Take a step back. Think about what's really going on. Assess the problem before jumping to a solution. And, even if problem-solving leads to the realization that content marketing *isn't* the solution, then that also counts as a win.

CHAPTER 5

The Problem-Solving Process

"How do you solve problems?" That was my opening question for every interview I did for this book. I generally got a deer-in-the-headlights response or, during phone interviews, total silence. Most people didn't know how to answer. They said something like, "That's a really good question" or, "I never thought about it that way."

However, once they had time to think about the question, they described following a process, which I agree is the right approach. They just hadn't realized it's the process they have been following. Here's a recap of the various steps people shared with me.

Step 1. Define the problem.

Defining the problem may seem an obvious place to start solving it, but it's surprising how many people ignore this step or give it short shrift. As discussed in the previous chapter, don't allow yourself to be distracted by symptoms. You must get to the root cause of those symptoms, which is the actual problem.

How the problem is defined has more impact than any

other factor on how—or whether—the problem is solved. Everyone involved, from the head of marketing to the marketing assistants, must agree on what the problem is. I highly recommend taking the time to write out the problem in the form of a question. It's a surprisingly helpful exercise for aligning a small group of people.

For example, you might write down, "People don't know our company, so they're not comfortable buying from us" or "Our clients don't believe what our sales team promises. How do we get that trust back?"

Be sure not to define the problem as a marketing problem. There are no marketing problems; there are only business problems that marketing can help solve.

In step one, you also need to identify the one or two metrics related to the problem. Are sales down? If so, by how much? Do you have a client retention issue? OK, how big is the problem? If the answer to such questions isn't clear, then you don't really have a clearly defined problem.

Step 2. Understand the impact of finding a solution.

What is the expected business impact of solving the problem? And, just as important, what do you expect to happen if the problem is *not* solved? This is the time to ask whether the problem is even worth solving. Although asking this question is counterintuitive, great problem solvers know when to step away.

If you sense that the effort required to solve the problem might exceed the value of the solution, have a conversation with your boss. You can frame it like this: "I've spent some time looking into this problem, and I suspect that the benefits of solving it won't be that great. I'm confident that I/my team can solve it, and here's what the effort would involve. . . . I think that our time would be better used to focus on other things. Do you agree?"

Thinking through and communicating the costs and benefits of solving the problem is not only a way to be sure the company is using its resources (that is, your and the team's time) well but also a way to find out how committed company leadership is to finding a solution. Clarifying the future beneficial impact of solving the problem also ignites the excitement of those tasked with applying their energy to solving it.

For example, if you're trying to solve a customer-acquisition problem, you need to outline the financial upside. Will a 5 percent increase in sales result in an additional $2 million in revenue per year? If so, all of a sudden, a marketing expense of $250,000 feels like more of a wise investment than an expense.

Without demonstrating the impact of solving the problem, your business problem might fade into the background as more pressing issues are addressed.

Step 3. Gather data and insights.

It's easy to be distracted by useless data, so sift through it and understand it. And then determine if the information is helpful or immaterial. If it's just anecdotal, for example, it could even be misleading. If you have access to technical resources, have them analyze the data with you.

A litmus test for evaluating data: "Does this data help us think differently? Will it take us in a different direction or lead to questions we haven't thought of asking?" That's the kind of information to look for. Fight the urge to look for data that support your preconceptions; they will just reinforce how you already think and won't help you think of other, perhaps better solutions. If instead you examine data purely to learn, you'll move closer to a good solution.

Step 4. Develop potential solutions using problem-solving techniques.

This is where the rubber meets the road. Developing potential solutions, usually the most challenging part of solving the problem, is more art than science. There's no guaranteed approach to developing solutions. However, you should be adept at a variety of techniques that will help you to develop potential solutions—including the five whys, root cause analysis, journey mapping, creative problem-solving, and Hurson's productive-thinking model. Part III, "Problem-Solving Techniques," goes into detail about each technique.

Step 5. Refine the solution.

Once you have a potential solution, the next thing is to determine its viability. Pressure-test the solution to understand any weaknesses. Try to poke as many holes as possible in the idea, even kill it. For example, if your solution involves purchasing $500,000 in media, is your company likely to approve that spending? If you need the sales force to have upgraded marketing technology, would the company invest in it? If the idea continues to stand up to your pressure-testing, then you know you're on to something.

When you think a solution is sound, provide the context of the problem and share the solution with your team members and the heads of groups that would be involved in implementing it, saying that this is one of the ideas you're thinking about. Don't expect them to immediately say, "Yes, that's a great solution"—which isn't what you want anyway. You want them to ask questions and poke holes in the idea. Their feedback will be extremely valuable to you; it will indicate how workable the idea really is.

How you present the potential solution to others is important. Don't appear to be excited, or even enthusiastic. Instead, present the idea as if you're unsure it will work. To get honest feedback, I say, "I think I may have a solution, but it doesn't feel right. Would you let me know what's wrong?" Phrasing it this way gives others permission to disagree with the idea. Creating a comfortable environment in which people don't feel pressured to respond in any particular way is the key to refining the solution.

Step 6. Document and socialize the solution.

After the idea has been pressure-tested and refined, you must do one more thing before implementing it: make sure that others are on board with the idea. This requires documenting it—that is, putting the idea in writing, so that it can be referred to later in the content-marketing process. Then share the solution with the appropriate stakeholders and decision makers.

This is pretty basic stuff, but you would be surprised how many people just tell people about the solution without putting it in writing. When presenting it to leadership for approval, keep the problem overview and proposed solution basic. You should be able to describe it in a couple of sentences.

When presenting it to people who will be involved in implementing the solution, provide more detail, including the data you used, the people you consulted or otherwise worked with, and the process you and your team used to arrive at the solution.

Getting buy-in requires working within your organization's hierarchy by managing up (to leadership) and down (to the team you manage) as well as horizontally, to colleagues and other interested parties.

Step 7. Implement the solution.

Implementation can be tricky. Sometimes, it will be as easy as hiring a company (see Chapter 24, "Different Ways to Create Content"), if you're one of those marketers who has the luxury of hiring an agency to do the content-creation work for them. Even if you do have that luxury, it's not always smooth sailing—you still need to oversee researching vendors, check references, get internal signoff, and do many other tasks. Other marketers are faced with having to add the work to their own—and others'—plates.

Beyond creating and implementing the solution, you also need to think about how easy it will be to roll it out both internally, at your company, and externally, with customers. Sometimes your solution will be well received and people will ask for it sooner. Other times, people are going to resist and slow things down because they don't understand or appreciate the value of the solution.

Sometimes you may be the only person involved in a solution. Other times, it may take a year to roll something out. For example, I once worked on a brand rollout that took about eighteen months to implement. On the other hand, I also worked at a company where the brand rollout happened literally overnight. Both companies were very large; they just had different approaches to change.

Step 8. Measure the effectiveness of the solution.

Even though measuring the effectiveness of the content--marketing solution that's been implemented is the last step, you should have been thinking about it from the beginning, when defining the solution. Be as clear and specific as possible about how success will be measured, so that you're measuring what really matters. Don't just say that an increase in website traffic, for example, will be considered a success and a decrease in it won't be. Instead, provide specific percentages.

After implementation, share the progress of the metrics with your team, your manager, and any other leader who should know about it. Tell them when the results will be in and deliver the information when it's available. Once you've reviewed the metrics and perhaps received feedback from customers or observations from your team members, you will know whether the solution is working and whether the implemented idea should be refined further. This ongoing optimization can take a good solution and make it better, or an underperforming one and make it viable.

One hopes that at this point the solution needs just a tweak or two. However, if the solution has not had the desired impact and you're unable to refine it so that it does, have the courage to walk away from the solution. Then start all over again to solve the problem, beginning with step one.

CHAPTER 6

Best Practices for Problem Solving

There's no clear path that guarantees that you will always be able to arrive at a good solution to a problem. And, even if a solution is found, there's no guarantee that a better one doesn't exist but hasn't been uncovered.

While there's no silver bullet for successful problem-solving, a variety of best practices help you think differently and increase the likelihood of solving the problem. The good news is that most problems are solvable. As John F. Kennedy put it in 1963, "Our problems are man-made—therefore they may be solved by man."

Use best practices at the first step, "Define the problem," and revisit them when you're stuck during the problem-solving phase. Notice that I said "when" and not "if," because you *will* get stuck. At times, you will be sure that no solution exists. It's not like arithmetic, where the same approaches are used over and over again to get the answers.

Here are six best practices to consider following. You might want to try them all.

1. Pretend you're the CEO.

On top of the other difficulties of problem-solving, you will face structural and political issues unique to your company. When you imagine that you are the CEO, the way you approach problem-solving changes immediately: you feel greater ownership of the problem, and your ability to solve it increases. Pretend you need to report back to the board of directors in a month with your solution. This instantly gives you the feeling you're empowered to solve the problem.

Adopting the CEO's perspective is also good because it forces you to think about the complete picture—about the best interest of the company, not one department or another. You're truly focused on solving the real business problem. This practice may strike you as silly, but, with some imagination, it can take you pretty far.

2. Get outside perspective.

Your instinct might be to try to solve the problem on your own or with only your team. However, don't limit yourself to those you work with every day. Get outside help—from people both inside and outside your company, perhaps marketers in other industries or even nonmarketers. Someone who isn't close to the problem can often see a problem more clearly and help you to see it from a new perspective.

I enjoy connecting with outsiders because understanding the context of the problem usually requires them to ask you questions. These questions are incredibly powerful because they help me to think in different ways. I've had many conversations in which I asked for an opinion, and the questions clarified for me an aspect of the problem—or the solution—and helped me reframe it. Such reframing has led to ideas I would never have come up with on my own.

For example, years ago, I had difficulties with a client who didn't see the value of what we were doing. Part of this was because the client had not been given a choice of agencies. A former colleague had some great advice: Ask the client to define the success of the relationship. Make him write it down. Then, share that definition so that everyone involved could be on the same page.

The relationship significantly improved because it made the client realize that his team was struggling to define success. Each of the ten-member client team had a different version of success. My former colleague's simple tip made all the difference.

3. Own it.

About a year ago, I backed up my car in a parking lot and headed toward a parked semi truck. The car has a warning system that beeps when the car is close to an object. The alarm wasn't going off, so I kept on backing and backing . . . until, all of a sudden, *crunch.* Turns out the warning system doesn't work for anything above three feet from the ground, which is where the bottom of the truck started. Since then, my car has had a small dent in it.

Why haven't I fixed the dent? Because I don't own the car; I lease it. In two years, I'll return it to the company, which expects there to be some wear and tear on the car. Does it make sense for me to spend $500 to fix the dent when it's not technically my car? Nope. No ownership, no investment in solving that particular problem.

Which of course leads me to the best practice number three:

own it. We don't think of many of the problems we encounter as our own. As soon as you take ownership of the problem, the chances of your solving it rise dramatically. Once you own the problem, it's hard for you to stop thinking about it until it's resolved.

Here's another example of how being an owner can help solve a problem. I worked with a notoriously challenging, yet effective, leader. He had a reputation for being really tough. He had multiple senior leaders working together on projects and it wasn't always clear who was in charge of a client issue or a pitch. Once he sensed that the team wasn't on track, he always appointed an owner, saying something like, "John, you own this problem now. If something goes wrong, you're the first person I'm going to talk to. You're responsible."

4. Frame the problem correctly.

Thomas Wedell-Wedellsborg is the coauthor of *Innovation As Usual: How to Help Your People Bring Great Ideas to Life.* In one of his problem-solving workshops, he asks you to pretend that you're the owner of an office building with tenants who frequently complain that the elevator is too slow. You need to solve that problem. Naturally, the first thing you think about is how to speed up the elevator. Do you buy a faster elevator? Do you upgrade the current one?

But what if you reframed the problem? Perhaps the elevator isn't particularly slow, but the tenants are annoyed because they *think* it's slow. If that's so, then the problem is the tenants' perception of their time in the elevator, not a slow elevator. How could you make their time in the elevator seem shorter?

Some people in the workshop suggested hanging mirrors on every floor opposite the elevator door. This solution would reduce complaints because people tend to lose track of time when looking at something fascinating—in this case, themselves.

Thomas's point is that how the problem is framed initially could lead to either a fixed or a brand-new way of thinking. Most people immediately think the solution to the problem with the tenants is to speed up the elevator in one way or another. But reframing the problem resulted in a simpler, much less expensive solution.

Once you think you've effectively framed the business problem you're trying to solve, challenge yourself to reframe it. Doing this early in the problem-solving process could take you down a completely different path.

5. Invite open-minded people.

Are you open-minded or closed-minded? You probably think you're open-minded, because an open mind is generally considered better than a closed one. But do you think that closed-minded people classify themselves as closed-minded? Probably not.

Who you surround yourself with is critical in problem-solving, and I can't stress enough how important it is for them to be open-minded types. They listen. They put their egos aside. Naturally curious, they want to figure out how to make things better.

Closed-minded people, however, can be poisonous to problem-solving. We've all been in a group that included one closed-minded person who completely changed the group dynamics. Sometimes you're not able to choose your teammates, so if you must work with a closed-minded person, think about different ways to engage him or her—perhaps in a one-on-one environment, separate from the group.

If such a person must be included in the team setting, however, talk to him or her early in the problem-solving process about the importance of keeping an open mind. When starting a team meeting, set the right tone by emphasizing the importance of keeping open minds. Such precautions could push the closed-minded person to try harder and improve how he or she interacts with the group.

6. Believe the solution exists.

Problem solving can drive you crazy. There's not a clear map of how to arrive at the situation. Sure, there's a process you can follow, or techniques to get you through the challenging parts, but the path to a solution isn't linear.

One thing that raises the odds of solving the problem is confidence that the solution exists, somewhere, waiting for you to find it. When stymied, continue to ask yourself questions, to uncover new information. Keep gathering different perspectives from other people. Continue to be curious. Be persistent.

Some of the most satisfying solutions of my career took weeks to find. For example, when I was working on change management for a brand project, my team wasn't sure how to tell whether those involved were taking the project seriously. So we created a brief quiz and tracked the results, a solution that helped us understand who was and was not embracing the project. (See Chapter 11, "Creative Problem Solving," for more about this solution.)

It's never easy to find the answer to a difficult problem. Sure, I often felt I was wasting time and going down paths to nowhere, but additional conversations led to new lines of thinking and, ultimately, solutions. Believing that I would eventually arrive at a solution is what kept me going. Nelson Mandela spoke to this phenomenon: "It always seems impossible until it's done."

Hold on to the knowledge that the solution is out there, just waiting to be discovered.

CHAPTER 7

Barriers to Problem Solving

How to solve a problem: Define it. Solve it. Move on.

If only it were so simple.

The bad news is that problem-solving, already difficult, is made even more so by a variety of obstacles that exist in our very own brains. The worse news is that we're not even aware of many of these cognitive barriers, which can slow down our problem-solving or even prevent it altogether. I guess you could call it unconscious incompetence.

Assuming that you and your team members are human, you are being held back by a number of factors, including those that follow. Being aware of them, however, can go a long way toward avoiding them, or at least minimizing their effects.

1. Unnecessary constraints

Draw three rows of three dots on a piece of paper. Without lifting your pen from the paper, use no more than four lines to touch all nine dots with your pen. Can you do it?

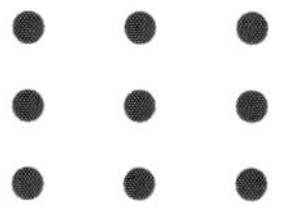

If it's the first time you've seen the nine-dot problem, the chances are you won't solve it. However, once you learn the answer, you will feel that it should have been obvious to you. If you couldn't solve it, it's because of something called unnecessary constraints—mental limitations that we inflict on ourselves—also known as functional fixedness.

When three U.K. academics conducted a study in 2001, they gave college students the nine-dot problem. Only 5 percent of the students could solve it, by drawing a line that went beyond the visual square created by the nine dots. Once you understand that you're not limited to keeping the line within the square, the odds of your solving this puzzle go way up.[11] See the illustration on page 271 to reveal the answer.

◆ ◆ ◆

I'm probably dating myself with this reference, but I loved watching the TV show *MacGyver* when I was a kid. Secret agent MacGyver could escape any situation by solving problems using his knowledge of science and engineering to make useful tools out of everyday objects. MacGyver certainly had no issues with unnecessary constraints. But most people do.

A few years ago, my team helped with a global webinar. Our role was to promote the event using social media, and we were brought in after the meeting logistics had been determined. The webinar logistics proved challenging because presenters called in from several different countries. During the practice session, everything went smoothly; the technology worked, and the

---

[11] Edward P. Chronicle, Thomas C. Ormerod, and James N. MacGregor, "When insight just won't come: The failure of visual cues in the nine-dot problem," *Quarterly Journal of Experimental Psychology*, Section A, 54(3), August 1, 2001: 903–19; https://doi.org/10.1080/713755996. See the article PDF for the solution.

transitions between speakers were seamless. During the webinar, however, people were obviously stressed out by the live event, and some presenters didn't do as well as they had in the practice session.

During a post-webinar recap the person in charge of the event asked, "Any thoughts or suggestions?" That's when I asked, "Next time, why don't we pre-record the webinar and do only the Q&A live?" Everyone sat there, puzzled: why hadn't they thought of that before? The reason is unnecessary constraints.

2. Mental set

In 1940, psychologist Abraham Luchins conducted a simple experiment. Participants were asked to fill one jug with water using only other jugs of water. After the participants completed the task, Luchins assigned the same participants the same task again, but this time he offered tools that would make the task easier. The second time, a majority of participants used the same approach they had used before. It worked the first time, so why would they need to change it? When confronted with problems to solve, we tend to focus on solutions that we've seen work in the past.

This lack of openness to trying new solutions is at the heart of why mental set can be a challenge to problem-solving. It limits one's ability to think of solutions.

3. Confirmation bias

Someone with confirmation bias unintentionally collects and uses data in a way that supports his or her preconceived notion. This bias causes the person to reinforce existing beliefs or values. Does everyone have confirmation bias? Yes.

Here's an example. You need to schedule four brief meetings on the same day, but there's only one hour when everyone who needs to be in those meetings can be there. What do you do? You probably choose the two most important meetings and set them up for 30 minutes each. You then reschedule the other two meetings for the next day. But why not have all the meetings during the same hour? Why not have four fifteen-minute meetings back to back?

The reason is confirmation bias. You automatically assumed that each meeting requires thirty minutes. But do you really need that much time? Probably not—fifteen minutes is plenty of time for most meetings. Confirmation bias prevented you from thinking of that option.

Here's another example of confirmation bias. You love playing hockey in a weekend league with a couple of your friends from Canada. A new co-worker transfers into your department from Canada. Attempting to be kind, you ask him, "Hey, would you like to play hockey this weekend?" He replies, "Thanks, but I don't play hockey." Your confirmation bias leaves you a little embarrassed, doesn't it?

4. Groupthink

Social psychologist Solomon Asch conducted his famous conformity experiment in 1951. Groups of eight college students were asked to participate in a basic task. But seven of the eight participants were actors, with full knowledge of the goal of the experiment, which was to understand the power of groupthink on decision making.

Each participant was asked to review cards with lines on

them. One card had one vertical line on it. The other card had three lines, labeled A, B, and C. The object was to match the single line with line A, B, or C. All eight participants, all in the same room, were asked to give their responses. Asch made sure the non-actor always answered last, after hearing what everyone else had said.

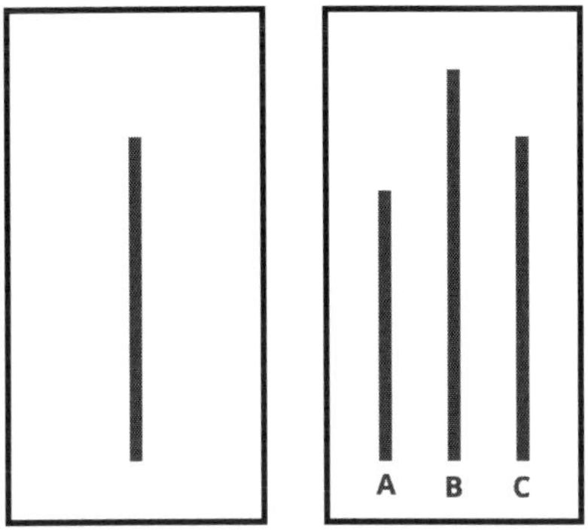

Each session consisted of eighteen rounds of matching. For the first two, everyone gave the correct answer. For the remaining sixteen rounds, actors were trained to give a wrong answer periodically. Even though there was really no debating the answer, the non-actor participants answered incorrectly 37 percent of the time. That shows the power that groups have on influencing decisions.

What does this mean for you? Be aware of how groupthink is affecting problem-solving and do what you can to keep a group from exerting too much influence on individuals, especially new members of the group. If you're leading a team, structure its meetings or problem-solving sessions in a way that minimizes groupthink. Instead of having one meeting with ten people, for example, have two meetings with five and compare the outcomes. Or, to eliminate groupthink altogether, have one-on-one meetings to see how each person solves the same problem.

5. Paradigm blindness

"That's never going to work."
"That's not the way we do it here."
"There's no need for that type of product."

These statements reflect paradigm blindness, which prevents people from seeing the possibilities of different solutions because they're limited by the current view.

Some famous people have been stopped by this barrier. For example, IBM chairman Thomas Watson once said, "I think there is a world market for maybe five computers."

Paradigm blindness is difficult to avoid because it's not easy to see. Visionary leaders, however, have a knack for overcoming it. Apple cofounder Steve Jobs, for example, always envisioned what "could" be created.

According to Henry Ford, customers are also subject to paradigm blindness. According to legend, he said, "If I had asked people what they wanted, they would have said faster horses."

6. Irrelevant or misleading information

Here's a riddle to solve. An airplane takes off from Canada and travels southwest. It is scheduled to arrive in Singapore in twenty hours. It enters international territory across the Pacific Ocean at a speed of 325 miles per hour. A flock of birds hits one of the engines, setting it on fire. The pilot immediately turns the plane around and travels east at 145 miles per hour. The pilot tries to return to the original airport but can't make it. The plane crashes on the border of the United States and Canada and kills most of the people aboard. The questions are: Where are the survivors buried? Is the airline responsible for the funeral costs, or should the funerals be paid for by one of the governments? If so, which one?

This famous riddle has been told for many years. Some people solve it right away. Others are misled by too much information and don't really hear the questions. They begin to think through the scenario and ask themselves questions. What nationality were the casualties? Shouldn't funeral expenses be up to the families? How many passengers had life insurance that would pay for funerals?

Of course, the answer to the riddle is that you don't bury survivors.

When you realize this is the answer, you feel cheated. You think, "You were playing a trick on me while I was really trying to solve the problem." This admittedly extreme example makes the point that often it's not easy to spot misleading or irrelevant information that needlessly complicates the problem.

The lesson here: beware of irrelevant or misleading information. This is especially true now, with increasing amounts of data surrounding us and threatening to bury us at an alarming rate.[12] Do your best to filter out the information that would not be helpful for solving your problem.

---

[12] According to the company Domo, "Over 2.5 quintillion bytes of data are created every single day, and it's only going to grow from there. By 2020, it's estimated that 1.7MB of data will be created every second for every person on earth"; www.socialmediatoday.com/news/how-much-data-is-generated-every-minute-infographic-1/525692/

part III

PROBLEM SOLVING TECHNIQUES

Think about when you were a kid. Can you think of a time when your parents or teachers taught you about problem-solving? No, I'm not referring to algebra homework; I'm talking about solving problems in general. If you're struggling to answer that question, it's because problem-solving isn't a subject that's formally taught in school or at home.

Once you understand each of the five problem-solving techniques described in this section, you'll possess a powerful collection of methods to help you solve problems, particularly the content marketing problems identified with the help of the last section.

why? WHY?
why? WHY?
why?

CHAPTER 8

The Five Whys

In the early 1990s, Washington, D.C., faced a mounting problem. I don't mean the first President Bush's budget fights with Congress or Vice President Quayle's spelling abilities. It started in May 1990, when a fifty-pound block of marble fell off the Jefferson Memorial building. Thankfully, no one was injured, but the problem required action at both the Jefferson Memorial and the Lincoln Memorial, which was also showing signs of falling apart.

Why was this happening? Were the memorials just aging poorly, or was something besides the passage of time causing the monuments to deteriorate? One plausible theory was that the chemicals used to clean the buildings were causing the deterioration.

But why did the memorials require frequent cleaning? Many starlings and sparrows congregated at the memorials, which required maintenance crews to frequently clean large amounts of bird poop off the building.

But why were so many birds flocking there every evening? Large clouds of midges (similar to gnats), providing perfect bird meals, could be found at both memorials at dusk.

But why were there so many gnats? It turned out that the lights shining on the buildings replicated the bugs' favorite mating conditions. In other words, the lights created the ultimate nightclub experience for the midges! Once the midges had hooked up, the females laid their eggs on the buildings—and it's really hard to remove midge eggs from marble.

To verify that the lights were the primary cause, U.S. National Park Service officials agreed to a six-week pilot program. The lights were turned on an hour later than usual only on Mondays, Wednesdays, and Fridays. Entomologist Don Messersmith and a team of students from the University of Maryland compared the quantity of midges at the Jefferson Memorial on those days with the quantity on the other days. On the days the lights came on later, 85 percent fewer midges appeared. Shutting down the midge nightclub almost eliminated the problem. Now that the U.S. National Park Service knew the root cause, it could solve the problem, by lighting up the memorials later in the evening.

The team working on the problem of the deteriorating memorials used the principle of a problem-solving technique called "five whys." Taiichi Ohno, of Toyota Motor Company, came up with the method, describing it in his 1988 book as "the basis of Toyota's scientific approach. . . . By repeating why five times, the nature of the problem as well as its solution becomes clearer."[13]

According to Toyota, Ohno encouraged the company's engineers to "observe the production floor without preconceptions. Ask 'why' five times about every matter." To demonstrate the method, Ohno used the example of a welding robot that stopped mid-operation:[14]

---

[13] Taiichi Ohno, *Toyota Production System: Beyond Large-Scale Production* (Productivity Press, 1988).

[14] "Toyota Traditions," Toyota Motor Company website, https://www.toyota-myanmar.com/about-toyota/toyota-traditions.

1. **"Why did the robot stop?"** The circuit has overloaded, causing a fuse to blow.

2. **"Why is the circuit overloaded?"** There was insufficient lubrication on the bearings, so they locked up.

3. **"Why was there insufficient lubrication on the bearings?"** The oil pump on the robot is not circulating sufficient oil.

4. **"Why is the pump not circulating sufficient oil?"** The pump intake is clogged with metal shavings.

5. **"Why is the intake clogged with metal shavings?"** Because there is no filter on the pump.

Here's an example from my own experience. One of my clients was a Fortune 500 manufacturing company. It owned several different brands, and the agency I worked for was responsible for updating the brand to better compete in the luxury market. The key component of the new branding was an all-new website that reflected the high-end positioning. Our team's design of the new website was very slick. Pursuing an affluent audience, we made some design choices that made it stand out. We were really proud of the site. The client was excited, too.

One of the primary metrics for measuring the website's effectiveness was user satisfaction, which was measured via surveys that users took after visiting the website. After the website launched, we couldn't wait to get our hands on the satisfaction scores. It almost became a contest among the team to predict how high satisfaction would increase: Would it go up 15 percent? Twenty-five percent perhaps?

But the results were ugly. User satisfaction went *down* 30

percent. Our excitement quickly became a sinking feeling. We had a problem to solve.

1. Why did user satisfaction drop so much? One theory was that any time a new website is launched, there is an initial drop in satisfaction.

2. Why does that happen? People are still getting used to the new site. That made sense, and we were hopeful the metric would rebound. But two months after the website launched, the numbers were basically the same.

3. Why were people still unhappy with the site? We looked at more data and noticed that the users of the customer-support part of the new website gave the site particularly low scores. This seemed understandable: perhaps they were upset because the company product they had purchased was broken and took it out on the company by giving its website low scores. But this turned out not to be the case—their scores were no lower than those of other users.

4. Why were the people who gave the lowest scores so upset? We saw that they tended to be older, not part of the young, more affluent audience we had built the site for. Apparently older people didn't like the site.

5. Why didn't they like it? Digging through the open-ended comments from the survey respondents, we saw complaints saying that the colors made the content hard to see and the text hard to read.

You see, in positioning everything as a luxury brand, we had used a black background on the website and made the text a little smaller than usual, to look sleeker and more distinctive. Our good intention, to redesign the content to be elegant, alienated older customers because they had problems reading the website. Once we finally understood that *that* was the real problem underlying the drop in satisfaction scores, we could fix it.

Among the many advantages of the five whys technique is that it's easy to understand; it can be explained in ten seconds. In addition, the technique is powerful; continuing to ask "why" often results in an eye-opening moment when the solution to the problem suddenly hits you. Another advantage of this technique is that it encourages teams to collaborate. Using the five whys works better in a group setting than individually, and the experience of solving a problem this way can be incredibly rewarding for the team.

The main disadvantage of this technique is that it doesn't always work. It usually helps the questioner to discover some new information, but it does not lead to a solution every time it's used—but then nothing works 100 percent of the time, right? In addition, people can become stuck and frustrated when the technique doesn't produce results quickly. And it tends to work better in manufacturing or process-oriented workplaces. This makes sense, since it originated at Toyota.

CHAPTER 9

Root Cause Analysis

Think of the story of the RMS *Titanic.* What's the first thing that pops into your head? Iceberg. But do you know that there were additional factors that led to the sinking of the *Titanic* and 1,514 deaths? Using a problem-solving technique called root cause analysis, we can identify at least five causes.

First, the ship was going too fast. Behind schedule and trying to make up some time toward the end of the trip, the captain ordered the engine room to bring the ship to full speed. Was the captain also eager to see how fast his new state-of-the-art ship could go? We can only speculate.

Second, some rare meteorological events occurred that year. The unusually warm gulf-stream water in the North Atlantic caused more Arctic icebergs to melt and drift southward into the area of the *Titanic*'s route.

Third, the helmsman initially turned the ship the wrong way. He thought that he had been told to "make the ship turn right," rather than "push the tiller right to make the ship head left." Even though the mistake was quickly rectified, the iceberg probably could have been avoided if time hadn't been lost because of the error.

Fourth, as metallurgists later discovered, the steel plates of the bow and stern were held together by low-grade iron rivets—perhaps because high-grade rivets were in short supply at the time, perhaps because the company that owned the *Titanic* was in financial difficulty. The hull would have ripped apart more easily with the low-grade rivets, causing the ship to sink faster.

Fifth, when the first officer ordered the engine room to slow down, it was impossible for the ship to slow down quickly enough. So he gave the order to reverse thrust, which caused the steering propeller to stand still for several seconds, making turning the ship more difficult. Even though the first officer thought that reversing thrust was the correct action to take, the seconds when no propeller was turning could have led to the ship's collision with the iceberg.

In addition to these five widely accepted causes, there are two theories. One is that second officer David Blair, who initially planned to be on the voyage and had the key to the storage compartment for the watch-tower's binoculars, was replaced just before the ship sailed. As a result, the people responsible for looking out for icebergs had no binoculars. That could have been kind of important, right?

Journalist Senam Molony has proposed yet another theory. He noticed in photos taken of the ship before it sailed a mysterious thirty-foot-long black spot on the ship's hull. According to Molony, there was a coal shortage in England at the time due to a labor strike. This forced management to find other ways to keep the ship's boiler running prior to the maiden voyage. Modern metallurgy experts say the wood-burning fire, rather than a coal fire, inside the ship could have weakened the hull by as much as 75 percent.[15]

---

[15]Rachael Pells, "Titanic sank due to enormous uncontrollable fire, not iceberg, claim experts," *Independent*, January 1, 2017, https://www.independent.co.uk/news/uk/home-news/rms-titanic-evidence-fire-senan-molony-belfast-new-york-southampton-sink-april-1912-a7504236.html.

Thus the seemingly straightforward story of the *Titanic* becomes more complex when root cause analysis is applied. Sure, the iceberg sank the ship. But understanding the many additional causes and possible causes of the disaster, provides a more complete and accurate picture of what happened. When you think about it, it's amazing how many things went wrong at the same time and contributed to the sinking of the ship.[16]

Root cause analysis was also applied to a different disaster, the *Columbia* disaster in 2003. The space shuttle *Columbia* broke apart while re-entering the Earth's atmosphere on February 1, 2003, destroying the spacecraft and killing its seven astronauts. The cause of the tragedy wasn't immediately clear. The investigation team had to study every aspect of the disaster to consider every possible cause. Video footage of the shuttle's takeoff—which had occurred sixty days before the disaster—revealed that a piece of foam insulation broke off the shuttle and grazed its left wing, damaging the heat shields—which are what normally protect the shuttle during re-entry. The eventual consequences of that foam hitting the wing were catastrophic. Thanks to the technique of root cause analysis, investigators concluded that this piece of foam's damage to the craft's left wing was the root cause of the disaster.

Now that you've seen root cause analysis in action, let's talk more about the technique. The best way to describe it is using the metaphor of a weed. The most obvious parts of the weed are the leaves, because they can be seen above the ground. But the leaf isn't the reason for the weed's existence; there's a complex system of roots beneath the surface that the weed wouldn't exist without. Root cause analysis breaks a problem down into its various parts, so that all the contributing factors to a problem can be understood.

---

[16]The literature on the *Titanic* is endless, including Alan Boyle, NBC News, "Ten causes of the Titanic Tragedy," April 1, 2012, https://www.nbcnews.com/sciencemain/10-causes-titanic-tragedy-62022.

The consulting firm ThinkReliability, described it this way: "Root cause analysis is about digging beneath the surface of a problem. However, instead of looking for a singular 'root cause,' we shift your problem-solving paradigm to reveal a system of causes. . . . Most organizations mistakenly use the term 'root cause' to identify one main cause. Focusing on a single cause can limit the solutions set, resulting in the exclusion of viable solutions."[17]

◆ ◆ ◆

Here's how to go about conducting a root cause analysis.

Step 1. Develop a problem statement.

The problem statement is usually pretty straightforward, but you need to write it down to make sure that it remains the focus of the analysis. In the *Titanic* example, the problem statement would be "The ship hit an iceberg, resulting in the death of more than 1,500 people." In the *Columbia* example, it would be "The *Columbia* disintegrated upon reentry, resulting in the death of seven astronauts."

Step 2. Identify multiple factors that contributed to the problem.

Start by identifying the sequence of events surrounding the actual problem. Ask yourself what happened before the problem occurred. Think about how far back to go. The low-grade rivets were used during the shipbuilding process, for example, long

[17] "What Is Root Cause Analysis?" ThinkReliability, https://www.thinkreliability.com/cause-mapping/what-is-root-cause-analysis/.

before the *Titanic* sank. And the root cause of the *Columbia* disaster occurred sixty days before the tragedy occurred. Identify as many factors as you can. Using the five whys technique here, to brainstorm multiple causal factors, can be very useful.

In addition, think about the values and culture related to the factors you identify. Which of the organization's beliefs allowed each particular factor to play a role in the problem? For example, in the face of financial troubles, it's likely that the company that owned the *Titanic* relaxed some of its materials standards to save time and money. And investigators of the *Columbia* disaster recommended that NASA make significant changes to its processes and organizational culture.

Step 3. Identify the root causes.

Remember why the *Titanic* watchman wasn't using binoculars? It was probably because he didn't have the key to where they were stored. Not having the key was one of multiple root causes. Once you think you've identified one of the root causes, there is an easy way to test if it truly is one. If you had been able to fix the cause, would it have eliminated the problem? For example, if the watchman had been able to use binoculars that night, would he have spotted the iceberg in time to avoid it? Probably. And if the piece of foam had not caused damage to the heat shield, would the disintegration of the *Columbia* have been avoided? In all likelihood. That's how you know you're onto a root cause.

Step 4. Connect the root cause to the problem statement.

Now that you have identified the root cause (or causes), go back to the problem statement you created in step one. You'll want to connect each root cause back to your problem statement. Using the *Columbia* example, it would go something like this: the shuttle disintegrated upon entry because the heat shield was compromised when a piece of foam came off and hit the left wing at takeoff.

Root cause analysis is a very powerful technique. It does take time, however. Don't be surprised if you find yourself frustrated while searching for the root causes of problems. You might even think there isn't a root cause to find. But keep on going. Eventually, your analysis will uncover what's really going on.

◆ ◆ ◆

Here's an example of root cause analysis that is closer to the business world. I used to work for a company called U.S. Satellite Broadcasting (now DirecTV). USSB helped launch the eighteen-inch satellite dish that has been popular for the past twenty years. When I started working there, we had about 500,000 customers (there are more than 21 million today). I worked in the corporate marketing department, in the customer retention division.

One day, the company's customer service call centers started hearing from a lot of unhappy customers complaining about their reception. Naturally, the call center reps thought the problem had to do with malfunctioning equipment, so they followed the protocol of troubleshooting over the phone to get the customer's satellite service back to normal. But the usual troubleshooting wasn't working.

What was really going on here? What was behind the problem?

It turned out to be solar storms. The technical term for these large emissions of energy from the sun is "coronal massejections." When this massive amount of energy hits the geosynchronous satellites that are more than 22,000 miles above the earth, TV reception suffers.

After solar flares were identified as the root cause of the problem, we handled customer communication in a completely different way. We proactively sent customers messages about approaching solar storms to explain what was going on and let them know to expect minor service interruptions. Once the customers understood why their satellite reception wasn't perfect, they could just accept having poor service for a day or two and move on.

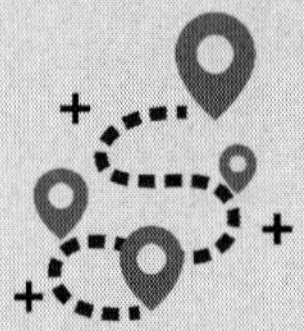

CHAPTER 10

Journey Mapping

We've all had poor customer experiences at some point, but some people have experiences that become infamous.

Perhaps you'll remember when the Amtrak customer was stuck in an elevator and tweeted @Amtrack asking for help. In 2016, Amanda Carpenter, the passenger, tweeted, "Guys. I'm trapped in an amtrak elevator at Bwi airport. Help?" More than six months later, Amtrak tweeted back, "@amandacarpenter We are sorry to hear that. Are you still in the elevator?" To which Carpenter replied, "Oh, my thank you for this but I was trapped months ago. Like last February. Thanks for checking? . . . Ha."[18]

In fairness to Amtrak, it had replied to the original tweet the same day Carpenter became trapped, and the later reply was a real-time response to someone's retweet of her original message many months later. But Amtrak couldn't control the story, and it became the poster child for poor customer experience.

Several years earlier, a Comcast technician had set up a modem in Brian Finkelstein's Philadelphia apartment.

---

[18]Ken Shepherd, "Amtrak Replies to Woman's Stuck-in-Elevator Tweet 7 Months Later: 'Are You Still in There?,'" *Washington Times*, September 7, 2016, www.washingtontimes.com/news/2016/sep/7/amtrak-replies-womans-stuck-elevator-tweet-nearly-/.

As part of the standard process, the technician phoned in to a Comcast regional call center to finish the setup. While left on hold for an hour, he fell asleep.

Finkelstein videotaped the snoozing technician, added music with the lyrics "I need some sleep. I can't go on like this," and uploaded the video to YouTube. The video went viral and news outlets picked up the story. Not a great situation for Comcast.[19]

Comcast isn't alone, of course. Many companies are caught providing poor customer experiences, and companies are often unsure how it happened. It usually happens because the organization has grown too big too quickly, and nobody has full ownership of the customer experience. The challenge in business isn't just understanding how to solve a problem, it's also identifying it in the first place.

◆ ◆ ◆

Journey mapping is an effective technique for identifying problems. Even though customer-journey mapping has gained more traction in the past five to ten years, its origins date to a 1989 book in which authors Chip Bell and Ron Zemke introduced the concept. They described it as a cycle of service mapping.[20]

The idea is to map out all the steps in a customer's journey from beginning to end—from the first time the customer first considers buying a product or service to when the customer has become the owner of the product or service. The key is to map the experience from the customer's perspective, not the

---

[19]"Comcast Moves to Cut Losses after 'Snooze' Video," *Deseret News*, June 26, 2006, https://www.deseret.com/2006/6/26/19960558/comcast-moves-to-cut-losses-after-snooze-video.

[20]Chip R. Bell and Ron Zemke, *Managing Knock Your Socks Off Service*, second edition (Amacom, 2007).

company's. The process is highly visual, and the final output is usually a large document. Only after the journey has been mapped out can you figure out how to improve it.

Customer-journey mapping can be done by an individual but is especially effective for teams. The technique provides a structure for organizing brainstorming or problem-solving sessions. I highly recommend that you have someone with journey-mapping experience lead the session the first time your team uses technique.

Following are the typical steps to creating a customer-journey map.

Step 1: Agree on what you're mapping.

The most challenging part of this technique is determining where to begin. Start with a specific type of customer and a specific journey. If the scope of what you're mapping out is too big, you'll never be finished with the mapping, so be sure to focus on a specific persona undertaking a specific task.

Step 2: Draw a timeline.

Draw a timeline from left to right. On the left side are the early stages of the journey, with the last stage on the right endpoint. Above the line are labels for the various sections of the customer journey. Common labels include awareness, consideration, evaluation, and purchase.

Step 3: Research the entire experience.

Talk to your company's actual customers and ask them to describe their journey. Ask questions like, "What's frustrating about this experience?" and "What would you do to make this a more enjoyable experience?" Ask them to go through all the steps they took, from first considering making a certain type of purchase to making the purchase from your company. Even if you think you know what the customer experience looks like, pretend you know nothing about it. You will be surprised when customers share some steps that you know nothing about.

Also talk to employees at your company who are familiar with customers' experiences. Your goal is to gather any information they may have about customer sentiment. They could have insight into why some of the internal processes are causing poor customer experiences, for example.

Step 4: Document.

Start filling out your journey map based on what you've learned from customers and colleagues. Use sticky notes, because there will inevitably be some back and forth with the steps. Also include all the customer touch points in the journey. For example; a customer's visit to a retail store, setup of an online account, or request for advice from a friend.

Step 5: Find the pain.

After the steps of the journey are mapped out, add to the map indicators of the customer's emotional state or pain points. These will help you to identify the parts of the journey that are broken—that is, the points at which customers experience difficulties. After you understand what's broken in the process, then you can move on to the next step.

Step 6: Identify improvements.

This is where the value of journey mapping really occurs. You've mapped everything out and understand what's causing your customer pain or frustration. Your team is now focused on answering the following questions: How do we make this better? How do we eliminate the pain?

You can do this in a variety of ways. Sometimes it involves fixing an internal process. Other times it might mean changing what and how you're communicating to your customers.

◆ ◆ ◆

In addition to revealing how the customer journey can be improved, journey mapping can be used for setting customer expectations and thereby providing a better customer experience.

For example, the contractor my wife and I used for our house's recent kitchen renovation understood his customers' journey and early on provided a piece of content that clearly laid out the different stages of a kitchen remodel—planning, design, demolition, installation, etc. The document showed customer sentiment that was typical at each stage. It showed excitement at the beginning of the project and immense frustration after demolition. At the end, it showed customer excitement again.

When, a couple weeks after demolition, we started feeling as if the kitchen would never be done, we remembered the map and thought, "Oh yeah, this is actually what we're supposed to be feeling." The contractor had done nothing to change what happened during the renovation; he had just set our expectations by letting us know that we would eventually feel frustrated and that, when we did, we knew not to worry because it was normal.

Journey mapping is inexpensive but can be challenging, because it's qualitative rather than quantitative. There is no exact science to creating journey maps, and every map looks different.

When using this technique, don't become obsessed with mapping out every detail. Stay focused on the big picture, continually asking yourself what an improved customer experience would look like. Have you eliminated the pain the customer is experiencing?

CHAPTER 11

Creative Problem Solving

There's a fable about the power of creative problem-solving (CPS). It goes something like this:

> *Many years ago, in a small Indian village, a farmer owed a large sum of money to a village moneylender. The moneylender, who was old and ugly, fancied the farmer's beautiful daughter, so he proposed a bargain: he would cancel the farmer's debt if he could marry the farmer's daughter. Because both farmer and daughter were horrified by the proposal, the moneylender suggested letting providence decide the matter. He explained that the girl would pick a pebble out of a money bag containing a black pebble and a white pebble. If she picked the black pebble, she would become his wife and her father's debt would be forgiven. If she picked the white pebble, she need not marry him and her father's debt would still be forgiven. If she refused to pick a pebble, her father would be thrown into jail. As they talked, the moneylender bent over to pick up two pebbles from the pebble-strewn path they were all standing on. The sharp-eyed girl noticed that he had picked up two black pebbles and put them into the bag. He then asked her to pick a pebble from the bag.*

With this understanding of the girl's dilemma, how would you solve the problem? Sure, you could expose the moneylender as a cheat, but that would likely only create a tense situation rather than resolve the situation. Think for a moment about how to solve the problem before reading the rest of the fable. Traditional thinking won't help.

> *The girl put her hand into the moneybag and drew out a pebble. Without looking at it, she fumbled and let it fall onto the pebble-strewn path, where it was lost among all the other pebbles. "Oh, how clumsy of me!" she said. "But never mind, if you look in the bag for the one that is left, you will be able to tell the color of the pebble I picked."* [21]

The girl used creative problem-solving to get out of a difficult situation. Her technique made it impossible for the moneylender to cheat.

Here's another tale of creative problem-solving, "The $10,000 Loan":

> *A Russian businessman walked into a Swiss bank in Geneva and requested a $10,000 loan. He offered to leave his Mercedes there as collateral, and the bank manager approved the loan. A year later, the Russian came back, repaid the loan and the 10 percent interest, and said he was ready to collect his car. The puzzled bank manager dared to ask him: "Excuse me, sir, but could you tell me: Did you really need that $10,000 so badly? In order to get the money, you left your luxury car with us for a whole year!" The Russian replied, "Where else in Geneva could I find such a great parking place for just $1,000 a year?"* [22]

Alex Osborn, founder of the Creative Education Foundation, developed the Osborn-Parnes creative problem-solving

---

[21] Many versions of this story exist, among them https://www.centerforcalmliving.com/a-tale-of-two-pebbles/ and https://www.48days.com/theres-always-another-solution/.

[22] Many versions of this story exist, including http://1world1way.com/coach/ww_russsia_humor.html.

process with Sidney Parnes in the 1950s. You may not be familiar with those names, but you've applied their work before. For example, Osborn coined the term "brainstorming," probably the most popular technique in problem-solving today.

According to the Creative Education Foundation, two assumptions underlie the Osborn-Parnes creative problem-solving process. First, everyone is creative in some way; second, creative skills can be learned and enhanced over time. The four principles required for the effective use of this technique are outlined on the foundation's website and quoted verbatim here:[23]

Principle 1: Divergent and convergent thinking must be balanced. Keys to creativity are learning ways to identify and balance expanding and contracting thinking (done separately), and knowing when to practice them.

Principle 2: Ask problems as questions. Solutions are more readily invited and developed when challenges and problems are restated as open-ended questions with multiple possibilities. Such questions generate lots of rich information, while closed-ended questions tend to elicit confirmation or denial. Statements tend to generate limited or no response at all.

Principle 3: Defer or suspend judgment. As Osborn learned in his early work on brainstorming, the instantaneous judgment in response to an idea shuts down idea generation. There is an appropriate and necessary time to apply judgement when converging.

Principle 4: Focus on "Yes, and" rather than "No, but." When generating information and ideas, language matters. "Yes, and" allows continuation and expansion, which is necessary in certain stages of CPS. The use of the word "but"—preceded by "yes" or "no"—closes down conversation, negating everything that has come before it.

[23]Creative Education Foundation, www.creativeeducationfoundation.org/creative-problem-solving/.

Of all the problem-solving techniques discussed in this book, this one is hardest to describe. In simple terms, the expression "think outside the box" comes to mind, but it's not that easy. Here's how the model works, according to the Creative Education Foundation, with six steps spread across four stages.

Stage 1: Clarify.
Step 1: Explore the vision. Identify your goal, desire, or challenge.

Step 2: Gather data. Describe and generate data to enable a clear understanding of the challenge.

Step 3: Formulate challenges. Sharpen awareness of the challenge and create challenge questions that invite solutions.

Stage 2: Ideate.
Step 4: Explore ideas. Generate ideas that answer the challenge questions.
Stage 3: Develop.
Step 5: Formulate solutions. To move from ideas to solutions. Evaluate, strengthen, and select solutions for best "fit."

Stage 4: Implement.
Step 6: Formulate a plan. Explore acceptance and identify resources and actions that will support implementation of the selected solution(s).

Even though the creative problem-solving process has this structure, there are no specific techniques or diagrams to follow. This explains why so many people have modified this framework over the years. The process has evolved into "the CPS Learner's Model," which includes additional concepts such as imagery and visualization.

When I worked for global risk management company Aon, I was tasked with developing and rolling out a new brand to the firm's communication teams and 500-plus marketers who were based in various business units and regions.

Here was a chance to apply creative problem-solving. First our team explored some of the more obvious solutions, but they all had significant impediments. We thought about creating a global-brand creative submission process, but the global team didn't have the bandwidth to review the submissions, and the process would slow down the business units. We could have the global team do a majority of the creative work, but this was an unrealistic solution, because business units wouldn't want to give up control and the global team couldn't support the language needs of seventy-plus countries. We also thought about having regional creative teams report to the global brand team, but at the time, structural and political issues impeded such a solution.

Given these issues, our challenge was to push forward the new brand's adoption in a way that required no changes to firm structure or organizational reporting. We had to build in some carrots and use the firm's executive team to help us enforce the changes.

In addition to creating a 200-plus-page brand manual that included templates and assets that teams could customize, our team used the four principles of creative problem-solving to come up with two ideas that became instrumental in making changes.

The first was building a brand quiz that every marketing and communications professional was required to take after attending a training session. They had to get a score of 85 percent to become officially "brand certified." What happened if they didn't pass the test? They had to take it again. The online quiz-platform we used provided analytics about every team member. The quiz results became the proxy for the progress made in each market. We worked with the top seven regional marketing leaders of the company, whose conversation turned to how many people on their teams had passed the quiz. Some people were really into the quiz and had fun earning an official certificate, while others thought it ridiculous—we often heard, "You're really going to require us to take a test?" Although it seemed silly to some, it was the only way to find out if people were paying attention to the training. Without the quiz results, we had no way of knowing if people understood the magnitude and the specifics of the changes they would be required to implement.

The other creative problem-solving idea for monitoring adoption was the creation of a central brand hub. Perhaps this seems obvious, but it hadn't been done in the past. Beyond having all the brand assets in one place, there was another reason we used the portal. We used single sign-on to track everyone who went to the site to download training documents, files, and videos. In other words, we could tell who was, and who was not, using the new brand assets.

Our team's conversations with firm leaders included data about who was accessing the brand portal. If a regional marketing leader told us that everything was going fine with implementing the new brand in his or her market (which is what most regional marketers told corporate), we checked the analytics to see if the story matched up. You can imagine the reactions when we said something like, "The team members in your business unit haven't even accessed the brand portal yet. How could everything be going well?" Once they understood that these analytics were available to the global team, and were being shared with the CEO, the leaders took the project more seriously, understood what success looked like, and made sure it was achieved.

Without the utilization metrics from the brand hub and the post-training quiz results, it would have been much harder, perhaps impossible, for our global team to manage change throughout the company. The solutions weren't obvious, and they helped the company evolve toward more consistently branded communication.

CHAPTER 12

Hurson's Productive-Thinking Model

Do you know the story of how Archimedes determined that King Hiero II was given a fake gold crown? Here's a hint: he didn't perform chemical composition analysis at the CSI crime lab. It was around 200 BC, so mathematician and all-around genius Archimedes solved it by making a connection between two seemingly unrelated things: water and the ways different materials behave.

It seems like the determination of whether a crown is fake would be a straightforward process, right? Just melt the crown and examine it. However, if the crown is real gold, then you've just wasted a perfectly good crown. The problem for Archimedes was how to prove the crown was fake without destroying it.

Archimedes's inspiration for the solution to this problem came in the bathtub—upon which he ran naked in the streets while shouting, "Eureka!" He realized that his body displaced water when he got in the tub—and theorized that different materials displace water at different levels based on their composition. He proved the theory by dropping silver into a vessel of water and then dropping the same volume of gold into the same amount of water. The two metals displaced different amounts of water. Testing the crown this way confirmed that the crown maker had diluted the gold in the crown with silver.

This story demonstrates that problem-solving isn't always straightforward. You can develop solutions by connecting factors in unexpected ways. Who would have thought displaced water could be applied to determining the authenticity of a king's crown?

Here's a more recent story of how a problem was solved by unexpectedly connecting two unrelated ideas. In the late 1970s, hundreds of thousands of people in India were needlessly blind from cataracts, a very treatable condition. Ophthalmologist Govind Venkataswami (known as Dr. V) wanted to eliminate blindness caused by cataracts, but he didn't have the time or resources to treat everyone.

One day, while he was watching a chess master play twelve opponents simultaneously, it hit the doctor: "Why can't I treat people for cataracts in a similar way?" Pursuing a solution, he traveled to the United States to learn from automotive and food manufacturers about mass production.

Back in India, Venkataswami opened the Aravind Eye Hospital, where he treated patients at scale. He made it affordable by charging one-third of his patients the full price and subsidizing the remaining two-thirds, who couldn't afford the surgery. An ingenious approach.

Today, Aravind is the largest single provider of eye surgery in the world. In 1998, its hospitals had 1.2 million outpatients and performed 183,000 cataract operations. Since opening in 1976, Aravind has restored sight to more than one million people in India. All because of the unexpected connection the doctor made between a multitasking chess master and ophthalmology.[24]

---

[24]Also see YouTube video "Infinite Vision," September 24, 2018; and Harriet Rubin, "The Perfect Vision of Dr. V," *Fast Company*, January 31, 2001, https://www.fastcompany.com/42111/perfect-vision-dr-v.

Tim Hurson, the founder of the productive-thinking model, believes that the power of making unexpected connections isn't realized by chance and has built a model that helps to make it happen.

The premise of Hurson's approach is that solving big, complicated problems requires one to think in radically different ways. He says that people tend to ask themselves the wrong questions. For example, they ask questions they already know the answers to. After all, it's harder to ask questions you don't know the answers to, but that's how the magic happens.

Hurson's productive-thinking model encourages creativity, which makes finding good and useful solutions more likely. But the technique goes beyond the free flow of ideas, as in brainstorming. There's more structure. You ask many defining questions at the beginning. You also determine what success looks like before you develop any ideas or solutions. Here's how it works.

Step 1. Ask what's going on.

There are several questions to ask, including the following:

- What is the problem? What is the question?
- What is the impact of this possible problem?
- What information do we already have? What information do we need?
- Who is already involved in the problem or question?
- What is the vision of the situation, and what does the target future look like?

Step 2. Ask what success is.

This step is about visualizing success. By defining it in

advance, potential solutions can be assessed more effectively. To define success, Hurson uses an acronym called DRIVE, which stands for *d*o, *r*estrictions, *i*nvestment, *v*alues, and *e*ssential outcomes: What do you want the solution to do? What are the restrictions? What resources are available to achieve your objective? What values must this objective deliver? And what outcome must it have?

Step 3. Ask what the question is.

This step distills everything in the first two steps down to powerful questions, what Hurson calls "catalytic questions," which help to focus the person (or team) who is solving the problem. It can be one or several questions—questions to which you don't already have the answers. These are the questions that force you to take a step back and think really hard. Sometimes coming up with these questions is just as hard as finding the solution. Getting as many answers as possible to the catalytic questions increases your chances of success.

Step 4. Generate answers.

At this stage, you start to generate multiple ideas and create lists of ideas and answers to choose from. It's important to note that you don't need to develop a finalized solution at this stage; you're just establishing a collection of ideas.

Step 5. Forge the solution.

In the fifth step, you eliminate some of the ideas that were generated in step four and develop the most viable ones into a solution. This is the time to compare the ideas with the success criteria that were established in step two. It's also the time to socialize the solution, refining it as people react to it.

Step 6. Align resources.

The last step of Hurson's productive-thinking model is about understanding the resources required to bring the idea to life. At this point, you are no longer ideating or pressure testing ideas. You're thinking through all the different things that have to be done, the order in which they must be done, and the resources that will be required to do them. This step can take some time, but it's very important. When you map out how you plan to implement the idea, people will have more confidence in it as a solution.[25]

◆ ◆ ◆

For a modern-day example of using the productive-thinking model to solve a problem, I spoke with Sarah Kennedy, the chief marketing officer (CMO) of software company Marketo, about how her team approaches problem-solving. Sarah's team was tasked with developing a theme for Marketo's annual conference, which in the software world is a big deal. Companies like Marketo invest millions of dollars in these multiple-day events to impress prospects and customers.

The team was struggling with how to position the event and its materials. Without a substantive theme that ties everything together, it's virtually impossible to organize conference

---

[25] For more about Hurson's productive-thinking model, see the video of Tim Hurson's TEDx-Maastricht talk, "The Shock of the Possible," April 7, 2011, https://www.youtube.com/watch?v=62PgFb2cXSg.

content and find speakers. (Companies usually fall into the trap of talking about themselves, which isn't much fun for attendees.) The core team was working hard but getting no traction.

So the CMO assembled a group of marketers to solve the problem. They agreed that the event's theme shouldn't be about Marketo; it should be about its customers. The group came up with an idea called the Marketo Fearless 50—fifty people in the industry who were thriving while using Marketo's software.[26]

Once the team landed on the idea of the Fearless 50, everything else fell into place. Taking the idea a step further, Marketo created a process for nominating oneself or a co-worker to the Fearless 50. A nice aspect of the idea is that it provided a whole new publicity-generating vehicle. When each of the nominees talked about his or her nomination to the media, Marketo received extra coverage on social media. This extra engagement created more awareness of the event and helped to identify the individuals in the final Fearless 50.

While the Marketo team didn't use all the steps in Hurson's model to solve its problem, it followed many of its steps.

It's not too surprising that companies don't use a structured process to develop solutions. But if you were to ask someone what steps they took to solve a problem, many of those steps would match those of Hurson's model.

---

[26]"Calling the World's Boldest Marketers to Join the Marketo® Fearless 50," Marketo news release, March 8, 2018, www.marketo.com/newsroom/press-releases/2018-03-08-Calling-the-Worlds-Boldest-Marketers-to-Join-the-Marketo-R-Fearless-50/.

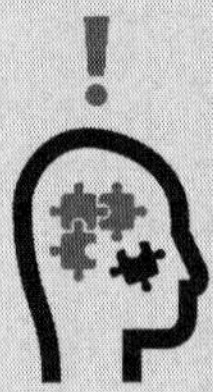

part IV

GROUNDING EVERYTHING IN A BUSINESS PROBLEM

Using the techniques discussed in Part III, you have identified the actual problem you need to solve. This section covers seven common problems marketing teams face: generating leads, converting prospects, onboarding customers, improving retention, changing customer perceptions, launching a marketing campaign, and getting referrals. How to create marketing programs to solve each of these problems is broken down, step by step.

CHAPTER 13

How Do I Generate Leads?

Customer acquisition is the lifeblood of most businesses, and it requires dedication and perseverance. In my experience, the more specific the audience being pursued is, and the more focused the corresponding content marketing campaign is, the more successful lead generation will be.

The most common way to initially identify the audience of potential new customers is to determine whether you are looking at the marketplace vertically or horizontally. Vertically means by industry—for example, construction, aerospace, or manufacturing. Horizontally means specific job functions—for example, marketing, engineering, or sales—regardless of the industry the functions are in.

It's possible to further define the audience by combining the two approaches, to target people in a specific niche—for example, accountants who work in the aerospace industry or IT buyers employed by professional services firms. Generally speaking, the smaller the company, the more preferable it is to combine the horizontal and vertical approaches. Larger companies are more likely to have specific teams or divisions that pursue particular niches, so that the company can pursue multiple niches at the same time.

You also need to identify the size of the companies where the people you want to pursue are employed. Generally, these are the four principal sizes of companies:

- **Large enterprises**—those with revenue of more than $1 billion per year and 1,000-plus employees
- **Midmarket companies**—revenue of $10 million to $1 billion per year, 101 to 500 employees
- **Small businesses**—revenue of $5 million to $10 million per year, one to 100 employees
- **Emerging market companies**—companies in the early stages of fast growth

In addition, you need to consider where the target audience is located. Are you going to target a specific state or region, or is your audience a national, or even international, one?

Finally, you must consider the job titles of the target audience. For example, if the product you're marketing has been developed for IT departments, titles to target might include chief technology officer, chief information officer, technology vice president, IT vice president, and IT manager. Or, if the product would interest only the top management of the IT function, you would target only the chief technology and chief information officers.

To sum up step one, to define the audience that your content-marketing campaign will target, ask yourself the following questions:

- Am I going after a specific horizontal, a specific vertical, or both?
- What business size or sizes are we targeting?
- Is our focus on a specific geographic area, a national audience, or an international audience?
- What are the likely job titles of those we're targeting?

A word of caution before moving on. Does your target audience want or need your product or service? Such a basic question, right? You would be surprised how often it is not asked. If the answer is "I'm not sure," the rest of the lead generation process will be frustrating and probably unsuccessful. Even when all the lead generation steps are followed carefully, the audience might not respond to the marketing effort. So, before going any further, be sure that the audience you're targeting is the right one for your product or service.

Once you're confident that those people being targeted are likely to want the product or service your company provides, continue with the steps for generating leads.

Step 2. Develop marketing personas.

After you've identified the audience to target, you need to understand what's important to them and how they make decisions. This is done by developing marketing personas. A persona is a tool that allows marketers to gain more knowledge about specific segments of the target audience. Each persona represents a group of people that is a subset of the audience you have targeted. The knowledge comes through discovering these people's needs, pain, interests, and decision-making journey. (See Chapter 13, "How Do I Generate Leads?," for additional information about personas.)

Building personas is important because they become the foundation for deciding what your content marketing consists of. Remember, the focus of your content marketing, at least at first, is your audience and not your company. Your content needs to demonstrate identification with the pain your audience faces. Then, once the audience sees that your company has acknowledged and understands that pain, the company will start to earn their trust. This trust gives you the permission to—eventually—talk about how your company can help solve their problems and relieve their pain.

When developing personas, don't make these common mistakes:

- Getting caught up in perfecting every little detail (there's no such thing as a perfect persona, just a general representation of a typical customer).
- Making a bunch of assumptions (if you don't know the target audience's real desires, needs, and wants, your marketing will be flawed, because it won't resonate with the audience).

The most useful and effective personas come from understanding your audience through one-on-one conversations with existing customers. By speaking with only five to ten people, you'll begin to see what they have in common. I always learn new things about the customer from having these conversations and developing personas. The insights I've uncovered through interviews have gone a long way toward shaping the content and the methods of its delivery. When responding to open-ended questions, customers take the marketer down paths that lead to new information and insights.

Here are some open-ended questions to ask during those conversations:

- What does your typical day look like?
- What are the challenges you face?
- What does success look like to you?
- How is your job success measured?
- How do decisions get made at your company?
- What frustrates you on the job?
- Where do you find information about your industry?

The number of personas you need to develop depends on how many personas there are within your targeted audience. It may be appropriate for your content marketing campaign to target just one persona—say, someone who is an IT manager at a professional services firm. It's more likely that you'll target multiple personas—at professional services firms, for example, IT leaders who are decision makers, IT managers those who are influencers, IT engineers who implement software, and those on the IT procurement team. After talking to enough people, you will start to identify different buckets and who goes in which one.

Step 3. Source the list.

When you know your audience and its needs, it's time to build the list of individuals to whom you will market your company's product or service. There are many ways to do this, but I prefer to develop a list using LinkedIn. The professional network contains rich data that tends to be relatively high quality and up to date. It provides the ability to see how you are connected to each individual, and its cost is low. For less than $100 a month, marketers can use the site's tool called LinkedIn Sales Navigator to build their target audience list.

Among the more popular search filters available on LinkedIn are people's industry, geography, seniority level, function, title, years of experience, company type, and company headcount. Tools such as Sales Navigator allow you to build a list in minutes. For less than $100 a month, you can go from having no idea who your customers are to being equipped with a list of details about prospective customers—and knowing how to connect with them. Pretty amazing, right?

If you don't go the LinkedIn route, there are other companies that provide similar types of customer data, though they are likely to be more expensive and to take longer. Some more well-established ones include Dun & Bradstreet (D&B), Demandbase, Zoominfo, and Experian. According to D&B, when choosing your list provider, look for accurate data, a comprehensive database, advertising network integration, and customer support.[27]

Bear in mind that you don't have to buy a list. You can organically develop your own by gathering contact info at an event. Another way to do it is to launch a traditional marketing campaign that generates a lot of traffic to a landing page that requires people to provide this type of information.

Step 4. Segment the list.

Let's say that you have built the list and have identified 5,000 potential customers. Next you need to find out which ones you or other people at your company already know. Why is this so important? Effective lead generation and nurturing is all about getting the attention of your prospect, and the easiest way to do that is by being introduced through a mutual connection.

Once you've gone through the list, split it into two groups: (1) people you or someone else at your company knows and (2) people you don't know and who have no connections at your company. Producing this final list is time-consuming because you must determine how you're connected to each lead. The best way to do this is by using a tool like LinkedIn's Sales Navigator.

If you work at a large company with several sales reps, there's

---

[27] "Find Customers Among the Clicks and Maximize ROI," Dun & Bradstreet, www.dnb.com/resources/b2b-audience-targeting.html.

a feature within Sales Navigator that allows people to tap into each other's networks. Once you connect your individual LinkedIn account to your company's account, you'll see another level of connectivity with your target audience. You can then ask your coworkers for introductions. This is called a second-level network request. It's very effective, because having a personal relationship with someone dramatically increases the chances of securing a meeting.

Step 5A. Approach the people you know.

Here, I'm not going into any more detail about approaching the people on your list with whom you or a colleague already has a connection. That's covered in the next chapter, which outlines how to convert more prospects.

Step 5B. Approach the people you don't know.

If you don't have a mutual connection with a prospect, you need to find another way to get his or her attention. This is the most challenging part of business development. Why? Virtually all prospects have been conditioned not to engage with salespeople. Don't be angry with your prospects. They're not to blame for this; rather, the volume of bad outreach that's happened over the past ten to fifteen years is. The number of companies that are doing outbound marketing has increased dramatically, and marketing automation tools have made it easy to send out messages at scale.

When I was in charge of global digital marketing at two Fortune 500 companies, my inbox and voicemail were always full of cold-outreach messages. I got three to five voicemails and twenty to thirty emails every day. I looked at all the requests but engaged only on the rare occasions when there was a good fit with my needs and unique outreach by the sales rep.

Unfortunately, to reach the group of prospects without connections to anyone at your company, you must spend some money on marketing or do some cold calling, and it's going to take a lot longer to connect with them than with the other group. What's the best way to do this? There's not an easy answer. It depends on a number of factors, such as your company's industry, reputation, and number of competitors as well as when prospects are in buying mode.

If during the persona-development step you asked prospects where they look for industry information or connections, then you'll have a place to start. I'm not going into how to reach these folks through paid media here because that topic could fill another book. However, some online channels to consider for reaching them are paid advertising (offline and online), search-engine marketing, sponsorships, affiliate marketing, and referral programs. If you choose to try to reach your audience online, be sure to explore advertising capabilities like dayparting (reaching your target at a certain time of day), geotargeting (targeting specific locations), and retargeting (sending follow-up messages to those who engaged with your ad or visited your website). Using these features will help you to create more effective campaigns.

Step 6. Put everything in a CRM.

Once you've identified your audience, by either building a list of individuals or using marketing to drive demand, you'll need a place to store the information about these people. That's why you need a customer relationship management (CRM) system. In simple terms, a CRM system allows you to store information about your customers. If you connect the CRM system to your website, you'll be able to track individual behavior online to each record. Having this extra level of insight is incredibly helpful. Not only will you know that one of the people on your audience list has taken some type of action, but you'll also know the specific pages the person visited. This knowledge helps you to focus on the most engaged prospects and customize future communications for them.

Most CRM systems have the same general cost structure. The more customer records you have, the more you pay. Some of the larger platforms are Salesforce CRM, Oracle Sales Cloud, and HubSpot. Some of the newer CRM systems are Infusionsoft, Soho CRM, and Drift. The good, or potentially bad, news is that if your IT department has already invested in a CRM system, then that's the one you will need to use.

Now that you have an understanding of how to generate leads and have a system in place to store them, we can move on to the next problem: how to convert these prospects into actual customers. The focus of the next chapter is how to use content marketing to nurture prospects and, ultimately, to help them buy from your company.

Notice how I didn't say "help you sell to them"? That's a key premise of content marketing. Even though everything we marketers do is in the interest of making a sale, content marketing is all about getting the prospect to choose to buy from your company.

CHAPTER 14

How Do I Convert More of My Prospects?

Every company needs to convert more prospects, because growth usually comes from new customers. This book doesn't explore many sales techniques. However, here I discuss how content marketing should complement the sales process.

Where do we start to find the solution to the problem of how to convert more prospects into customers? It all happens during the first meeting with a prospect. Is the goal of that meeting to provide an overview of your company? No, though that will come up. If you want to sell to more customers, the main objective is to know the challenges and pain points of your potential customers.

Even if doing so feels comfortable, don't share the same presentation with every prospect—it's a waste of time. To sell more, your company must overcome the particular problems of prospective customers. This is also the foundation of an effective content marketing program. How do you accomplish this? By taking the following steps.

Step 1. Identify the problem.

Traditional sales techniques push the company's perspective

onto the prospect. The same approach is applied over and over again. It's like an arm-wrestling contest in which your opponent must eventually give in and declare you the winner. Content marketing is different. Sure, the goal is to close the deal, but you're not trying to overpower the person. You're trying to get the prospect to buy your solutions to his or her problems.

To get prospective customers to buy from you, you need to offer a way to solve their problems. You've probably experienced this yourself in an interaction with a salesperson. You may have thought afterward, "I don't feel as if I was being sold to at all. I was in charge the whole time." In reality, you were being sold something. The salesperson was out front, leading you down a path rather than pushing you from behind.

What's the best way to uncover customers' pain? By asking good open-ended questions. Great salespeople ask great questions, such as the following, to uncover the pain:

- What's the biggest challenge you face in the next six months?
- If I gave you a magic wand, what's the one thing you would change?
- What's keeping your company from growing faster?
- What's the biggest challenge your customer faces?
- What intrigued you most about meeting with us today?
- What's your CEO's biggest challenge?
- What's broken in the relationship with your current provider?

When asking these questions, don't just get an answer and then move on to the next question right away. Ask several follow-up questions. Dig deeper. Sometimes it might take four or five follow-up questions to uncover the real source of pain. Think of yourself as a detective interrogating a suspect—in a nice way, of course.

Using this technique will give you essential insights into a prospect's pain. Sometimes, your questions can even lead the prospect to discover something that's new to him or her. You will hear things like, "Wow, I have never even thought about it that way. I guess that *is* my problem." Such a conversation earns you lots of points, because you are then perceived as someone who can deliver value, and it didn't even cost the prospect anything.

When done the right way, your first meeting will feel like a therapy session, with you as the therapist. You want the prospect to lie down on a nice comfortable couch, feel at home, and talk about his or her anxieties and describe the problems encountered on the job every day. Listen intently. Nod your head. Show empathy. The more the prospect understands you're there for him or her, the more the prospect will open up to you.

The goal of the first meeting is commonly described as "dragging 'em through the glass." You want your prospect to share all the pain his or her company is experiencing, and to extract that information, you want the prospect to describe all the terrible problems he or she is up against. As I've said before, the key is asking great questions.

When you have a good understanding of the prospect's pain, you can build trust by using what I call the "you're not alone" approach. Once it becomes clear what the pain is, tell the prospect that his or her problems are not unique, that in fact you've helped similar companies solve similar problems. Say something like, "What you're saying sounds similar to something we helped company X with." Sometimes this technique will be enough to secure your next meeting.

This point is an excellent time to share a piece of content with the prospect—which is why it's a good idea to have on hand case studies about how you've helped other companies. When you ask, "Would you like to see a case study on your issues?," it's hard for the person to say no. Sharing any piece of relevant content, whether a precisely targeted case study created by your team or an article from an outside source, is very helpful at this point.

You might be amazed to find out what's really important to your prospects. Sometimes you will discover that their pain points are completely different from what you had thought they were. And that's a good thing! Why? If you hadn't uncovered the truth about their pain, your follow-up activities would have been irrelevant. All of your follow-up communication and content should be based on what you have learned in that first meeting about the pain points of the prospect and the company.

Step 2. Build the content marketing plan.

Now that you have an understanding of the pain points, you can build your content marketing program. The first thing is to draw a timeline. On your left is where you are today. And the endpoint is a closed sale.

You now must ask yourself what content would show the prospect that we understand their pain and that their pain can be alleviated? You must consider the content to share in your next meeting with the prospect—and what content to share in between the meetings. You're essentially asking yourself what combination of content is most likely to convert the prospect into a customer—and, in the aggregate, what will have the biggest impact on the conversion rate?

Here are the three things that your plan must include, and that will be reflected in your timeline:

- What do you say to prospects at different moments?
- What type of content formats should you use to communicate what you're saying?
- How often should you communicate?

Bear in mind that there are usually no strictly right or wrong initial answers to these questions, because you'll have the opportunity to tweak these variables later in the process. You can only start with your best assumptions, based on your or your team's experience.

Step 3. Create the content.

How to go about creating the content is covered in Part VI: "Content Execution."

Step 4. Distribute and monitor the program.

Once the plan and timeline have been completed, you're ready to launch the program. This is the fun part, because you can see how the content is working in real-time, assuming you are using the right tools. Hopefully, you're using a CRM and web-management platform that shows how each prospect is responding to your outbound communication.

Any time you launch a piece of content on your timeline, you will know right away what has happened as a result. Did prospects open your email? Did they forward the email to anyone else in their company? Did they click on a link? Did they visit your company website? If so, how much time did they spend there, and what pages did they look at? Tracking these actions will let you know how engaged your prospects are with the content.

You are looking for an incremental rise in the conversion rate. You will find that some pieces of content work better than others, which will help you figure out how to refine the content-marketing program. Now I have some bad news for you:

You're never going to be done making tweaks. Improvements can always be made, of course, and some techniques or pieces of content that work at first will stop working later.

Use the tools in place to test various approaches. Experiment by changing one aspect of the program at a time for a subgroup of prospects. Perhaps you want to test the frequency of emails, the time of day they are sent, or the wording of the subject line. Perhaps you want to see if the audience prefers videos to article PDFs.

The goal of this testing is the eventual development of a control group of approaches that perform best. Companies that do a great job with this apply their winning content-marketing formula to 80 to 90 percent of their prospects, and new approaches are tested continuously using the remaining 10 to 20 percent of prospects.

Figuring out how to convert more prospects can be hard work. There are many factors to analyze: where leads have come from, the industry the prospects are in, how your content timeline looks, changes in the marketplace, and more. The list can seem endless. But with the aid of a content plan and timeline, as well as technological tools, you will be able to see what's working, make the appropriate changes, and convert more prospects.

CHAPTER 15

What's the Best Way to Onboard Customers?

Producing a TV show in front of a live audience has its challenges, among them booking high-quality guests, writing consistently funny material, and managing the production logistics. Studios are usually customized based on the needs of each show, to ensure the show runs as smoothly as possible.

Now imagine that you take your normal operation on the road, as Conan O'Brien does a couple times of year. How do you create a mobile version of the show's studio that will keep the show run smoothly on the road? That's where Nextiva comes in. It's a voice-over-internet-protocol (VoIP) company that focuses on cloud-based communication solutions. Put another way, it ensures that internal and external communication are seamless when the show has been uprooted from its studio.

Nextiva earns accolades for customer service. There's no secret to how they onboard customers. Yaniv Masjedi, CMO of Nextiva, said it very straightforwardly: "If we can provide a simple and effortless experience, we're going to win."

Nextiva has a team dedicated to onboarding. The team knows that the first hundred days are the key to long-term customer retention, but it's the first couple days that make the biggest difference.

Success requires more than a great onboarding team; it also requires having the logistics and operations in place. "Do what you say you're going to do," advised Masjedi. I wish more B2B companies approached their customer experience as Nextiva does—with no complex strategy, just great customer service and the right systems in place.

It's common for companies to put significant energy into the sales process, but most companies don't expend a lot of effort on onboarding. After a big sale, many sales and marketing teams relax and shift their focus to finding new customers. Great companies know not to do this.

The way new customers are brought on board constitutes an essential part of the customer experience. Ensuring a good experience isn't just the right thing for a company to do; it has an impact on the company's bottom line. According to research from the Temkin Group, a "modest improvement" in customer experience could have a big impact on a company. The group found that, on average, a $1 billion company "can gain $775 million over three years."[28] Consider that for a second: by providing a great customer experience, your company could generate an additional $400 million to $800 million in revenue for every $1 billion in revenue. Do I have your attention?

The company Regalix recently reported that customer satisfaction is the number-one benefit that organizations gain from well-done customer onboarding.[29] It's not easy, however. According to a report by consulting firm North Highland, the most common "failure points" during onboarding are the misalignment of functional areas, lack of communication, lack of understanding of customer needs, technical/system issues, lack

[28]Temkin Group, "ROI of Customer Experience, 2018," August 21, 2018, https://experiencematters.blog/2018/08/21/report-roi-of-customer-experience-2018/.
[29]Regalix, "The State of Customer Onboarding 2019," April 2019, "State of Customer Onboarding 2019," April 2019, https://www.regalix.com/insights/the-state-of-customer-onboarding-2019.

of information/data, and a lack of resources.[30]

In this chapter, I outline the steps you and your team should take to solve the business problem of how to give new customers a great onboarding experience and what you can do to overcome common challenges. Anyone following these steps needs to bear in mind a few guiding principles.

First, set the right tone early in the relationship. Naturally, the first couple of touch points are the most important ones. Customer relationships can be complex, especially when the number of people on the customer team is in the double digits. That's why there must be someone in the company being brought on board who is the clear owner of the relationship as well as a relationship lead in your company. These two relationship owners need to work together to create an effective onboarding road map, which lays out the activities required to give onboarding customers a great experience. Make sure the experience uses technology, but don't rely only on technology. Don't underestimate the importance of high-touch experiences; make sure the road map combines in-person meetings and personal outreach. If it doesn't, the relationship will suffer.

Cater to different learning styles; don't develop a one-size-fits-all program that works for only certain customers. Some people may want self-directed learning, while others prefer a classroom environment. Be flexible. Even if your company has a specific onboarding approach in place, confer with the customer in advance. Share the plan and ask whether any modifications would help increase the engagement of the customer's team.

In addition, make sure there's continuity between the sales and account teams. Nothing is more frustrating to a customer

---

[30] Todd Nisbet and Rob Sherrill, "Bringing Value Onboard: Optimizing the B2B Customer Onboarding Experience," *Harvard Business* Review Analytics Services Survey, August 2016, https://www.northhighland.com/insights/white-papers/hbr-north-highland-b2b-onboarding.

whose expectations aren't being met than a salesperson who vanishes after a deal is closed. The salesperson doesn't have to create or manage the onboarding experience, but he or she needs to be present at key meetings. And the salesperson should follow up with the customer to make sure the expectations set during the sales process are now being met.

The following steps to creating a great onboarding experience apply to B2B companies with dedicated account teams. According to the Regalix research, it takes organizations an average of three to eight weeks to bring a new customer on board.[31]

Step 1. Determine your onboarding approach based on relationship value.

It's good to take different approaches to onboarding based on the value of each customer. As a rule of thumb, for more important customers, bring in more senior members of your company and conduct a greater number of in-person meetings. If a customer lacks revenue or long-term growth potential, a scaled-back version of this approach is OK. Once the overall approach to a particular company has been determined, identify the team members in each company who will be involved. This is also the point at which one relationship lead from each company must be identified.

Step 2. Introduce the partnership.

Communicate to all involved that a clear onboarding plan is in place, as is a dedicated person in your company to lead it. Following up the announcement with a solid plan goes a long

[31] Regalix, "The State of Customer Onboarding 2019."

way with the customer. In addition to sending out an announcement email, your company's relationship lead should personally reach out via a phone call to each of the customer team members. This small gesture can also go a long way.

Step 3. Set up an official kickoff meeting.

This is your chance to orient your customer to your company. Who are the individuals on your company's team who will interact with the customer's team? What tools do they use? What is your company culture? Communicating this information upfront shows that your company has a certain way of doing business. It's not to say that you can't be flexible, but you definitely want to communicate that your company is really good at what it does and has a proven way of doing it.

Step 4. Share the onboarding map.

Make the different phases of onboarding and how long they take very clear to the customer.

Also consider making a big deal out of everyone on the customer team completing the onboarding process. Try to think of a fun way to recognize the accomplishment. Some companies hand out printed certificates; others throw happy hours or give away company swag. It doesn't matter how you celebrate; it's just important to acknowledge it. This recognition step is important because it gives the customer team members a clear moment to raise their hands and ask questions or express concerns.

Step 5. Set up rules of engagement.

What does your team do if something in the customer relationship isn't working? Who should be called if there's a personality conflict with the customer team? What expectations do the service-level agreements set? That's where the rules of engagement come into play.

Early in the relationship, your team lead should discuss with the customer's team lead how various potential scenarios would be handled. Having this clarity upfront is really important, so that everyone knows how to notice signs of something gone awry and when and how to escalate issues when necessary. The value of a relationship lead on both sides is that he or she becomes the clear point of escalation if something isn't working.

Step 6. Monitor relationship health.

What happens once the onboarding process is over? This is where it can get trickier. You may think everything is going well, but behind the scenes an issue or two may be lurking and building up—which is why your company's commitment to monitoring the health of the relationship is important.

On a regular basis, combine inbound and outbound tactics to gauge customer satisfaction with your company. I recommend starting with a one-on-one conversation, either in person or via a phone call. Ask the customer how things have been going and what can be improved. A more formal way to do this is through surveys. Consider surveying all your customers one or two times a year. (See the next chapter, "How Do I Increase Customer Retention?," for more about customer surveys.)

There are always ways to improve customer experience. The act of asking customers simple questions via a survey goes a long way. Be sure to make the questions open-ended, so what you receive from customers is more than numerical ratings or yes-and-no responses. Make them really think about the relationship between your company and theirs. Ask them what's been challenging about the relationship and what can be done to improve it. You might be pleasantly surprised at the quality of the insights you can glean from customer surveys.

Step 7. Make training and education ongoing.

After the onboarding is over, create and explain to your team and the customer team a plan for ongoing customer training and education, required as things at your company change over time. For example, it may add a new product or service to its offerings, the workflow may change, or there may be turnover of employees on either team. At a minimum, have an annual meeting of both full teams to keep everyone up to date.

Moreover, your company's customer-relationship team should hold similar meetings. Sometimes quarterly meetings of everyone on a relationship team are a good way to come together, share notes, review recent changes, and discuss how the relationship is going. With this information, the relationship lead can then take appropriate action if necessary.

One company that is great at discussing ongoing product news and information is monday.com, which provides to its customers a cloud-based project-management and collaboration tool. Usually once or twice a month, the company reaches out to teach its customers about new product enhancements, via live webinars or on-demand courses that customers can access any time. Monday.com also provides its customers with examples of how other companies have been using its software, via real use cases that help their customers get more value out of the tool.

CHAPTER 16

How Do I Increase Customer Retention?

There I was, standing in Chicago's Midway Airport, about to start a vacation from my job at Digitas. I had just updated my out-of-office voice-mail message (making sure not to have a boarding announcement in the background) when my phone rang.

It was the managing director of the Digitas Chicago office, who normally didn't call my cell phone. After an exchange of pleasantries, she cut to the chase. She had heard from Best Buy, our client for four years. After a long decision period, the company had finally decided which agency to move forward with. It wasn't Digitas.

A minute before, I had been excited to start my vacation, but this news was a huge buzzkill. It would have been a six-figure deal that supported a team of fifteen. The news was hard to process. Why did Best Buy go with someone else? What could we have done to retain the account?

In my daze, I noticed a woman in an airport convenience store looking for a snack to take on the plane. First, she picked up a bag of pretzels, and then she put it back on the shelf and picked up a bag of trail mix. Yep, that's the one she wanted. Without hesitating, she paid at the register, put the trail mix in her purse, and headed to her gate.

I compared the two decision-making situations: To make their decision, our client had taken a year and involved 100 people. The woman had made a decision in fourteen seconds. I smiled in appreciation of the stark difference.

Why am I mentioning the trail mix woman? It's an example that brings to life how businesses make decisions. On one hand, she considered the options and made a decision by herself in 14 seconds. Her thought process probably went something like, "I know they won't feed us on the plane, and I'm hungry. Oh look, peanuts, raisins, M&Ms, pretzels . . . trail mix!"

Although I'll never know exactly what the Best Buy team's process was before arriving at its decision, no doubt it involved gathering and weighing much more information than the trail-mix woman did. After all, it was a much weightier decision, with more money and the fate of many more people at stake.

As marketers, we need to understand as well as possible how people make decisions and what we can do to encourage customers to decide to stay with our companies.

I like to apply to decision making a model based on the premise that all change is filtered through three lenses: political, rational, and emotional. Regardless of how little or big the decision is, the decision maker's brain always uses one or more of those lenses when considering the various factors that will determine the decision.

For example, say you're on a team that's deciding which marketing firm your company will contract with:

- You are likely to consider the following *political* factors: Does anyone at my company have a personal relationship with the agency?

Which agency will make me look better internally? How much control will I have over the agency relationship? What will my CMO or CEO think of this decision?

- Looking at the decision through the *rational* lens is likely to raise factors such as: How much will using the agency cost? Does the agency have enough relevant experience? Which agency has better technology? Which agency can do the work faster? Where is the agency located? Is it financially stable? What are its payment terms? Will it be easy to work with? Do we even want to invest the time required to train a new agency?
- The more *emotional* factors might include: How do I feel about this decision? Which agency is the best cultural fit? Do I like the people at this agency? Will working with this agency make my life easier or more stressful?

When it comes to figuring out how to increase customer retention in the B2B world, the good news is that time is usually on your side. The length of decision-making cycles depends on many factors, but, in general, decisions are made within six-month, one-year, or two-year windows. Five-year contracts aren't rare, however, and some might lock in a company relationship for as long as five to ten years.

If you want to raise your company's customer retention rate, you need to be aware of what customers consider when deciding whether to continue to work with your company. Among the most common dynamics that determine customer retention are:

- The number of people involved in the customer's decision
- The customer's satisfaction with the current product or service he or she is receiving
- Value based on the price being paid
- Changes in the marketplace (new technology,competitor offerings, etc.)
- Changes the customer is undergoing (cultural, structural, technological, etc.)

With all these factors in play, how can you know what's really happening, so that you can make the appropriate changes that will make customers less likely to leave?

Generally speaking, here's how you can build out a content-marketing plan with the goal of retaining more customers. The key is not to start with content at all. Gather insights first.

Step 1. Put content into trackable formats.

A customer-retention plan starts with intelligence. Some information will come from good old-fashioned account and sales management, via those teams' ongoing conversations with the decision makers and influencers of customer organizations. This is the most effective way to glean insights into your customers.

But don't rely on human intelligence alone. Combine it with digital intelligence—that is, the insights you can gain from how the customer engages with your content.

Take two scenarios. First, let's say you're sending information about a new product to a customer in a PDF. You write an email, attach the file, and hit send. And then you wait. And wait. And wait. The customer might have opened the PDF attachment, perhaps she even read its content, but because the customer's responses can't be tracked, you won't know unless she takes the initiative to tell you.

In the other scenario, instead of sending a PDF, you put the new-product info on a website and send the customer a link to it. Or perhaps you put the PDF on a platform like Pointe Drive. Now you can see the customer's engagement activity. Did she go to the web page? Did she open the posted PDF? How much time did she spend on each web page? Did she even get to the pricing page? Because the customer's activity is trackable, many valuable pieces of information can be collected that will reveal how engaged the customer is.

A Fortune 500 company I worked for gathered intelligence this way. The company periodically sent emails with links to the content published on its website. Over time, the marketing people could see how each customer responded to each message. They could even track what the customer did after reading the content. For example, after viewing the content, did the customer click on a link to information about a product related to the content topic?

All of the data was compiled into an engagement index for each customer. The company then knew not only each customer's level of engagement but also the content formats and topics that the customer engaged with.

Why is this important? Because once a company knows the type of information a customer cares about, it can adjust its sales or marketing strategy to better connect with that customer.

Step 2. Examine the data.

Here's the really cool part. The Fortune 500 company mentioned in step one looked at all the collected engagement data and correlated it to customer retention. Customers who were highly engaged with our content were more likely to renew their contract with the company. This was huge, because now the company could predict which customers were more likely to leave. Months before the customer made its decision, his or her low content engagement would raise a red flag, so that we could create and put in place a plan aimed specifically at retaining that customer. This demonstrates the power of having the right content tools and content in place.

Here's another example of how to use engagement data to predict retention. When I was in charge of global digital marketing at Aon, we asked three agencies for proposals for a website redesign. One of the agencies built a microsite for the pitch team and posted documents on it. When the agency published new content, such as a relevant article they had created, we received an alert via email. Not only did this help the agency stay at the top of our minds as we decided among the agencies, but it also told the agency how many people on our team were engaged.

Contrast this approach with what the other two agencies did, which was standard outreach to us via emails and phone calls. They had no way of seeing how engaged we were.

Always put your content in a trackable format.

Step 3. Deploy surveys to gather further insights.

An additional step you can take to increase retention is to send a survey to your customers to find out how things are going. Conducting surveys isn't new, of course, but a specific type of survey for this situation has been the standard for a while.

In 2003, the *Harvard Business* Review published an article titled "One Number You Need to Grow." The title refers to a metric called Net Promoter Score (NPS). NPS has evolved since then, so that organizations all over the world now use it for measuring customer experience and as a leading indicator of business growth. The scores reflect customers' answers to a corequestion: On a scale of 0 to 10, how likely are you to recommend [Brand X/Company Y] to a friend or colleague?[32]

[32]Frederick F. Reichheld, "One Number You Need to Grow," *Harvard Business Review*, December 2003, https://store.hbr.org/product/one-number-you-need-to-grow/R0312C.

Why is using a survey approach like NPS, rather than a typical customer satisfaction survey, important? Because the NPS is a better predictor of the likelihood of a customer's renewing.

You may be wondering what NPS has to do with content marketing. A lot, actually. You can segment customers according to their scores and create a custom content marketing plan for each segment. After all, the message to customers who are enthusiastic about your company should be different from that to customers who are more likely to pull their business in the near future.

Setting up an official NPS survey can be complex. If you don't have the time or money to work with, I recommend creating your own survey and scoring methodology. It can be a short survey you send out using a simple tool like Survey Monkey.

Alternatively (and more simply), you can spend ten to fifteen minutes talking to each customer. Granted, this approach won't win you any research methodology awards, since the execution of your phone survey would be biased (see the example of the feedback-seeking chef in Chapter 17, "How Do I Change the Perceptions of Others?"). Nevertheless, you'll obtain some feedback that will help you understand where the customer's relationship with your company stands.

Step 4. Build a content marketing plan.

Now you know how technology can help to develop insights into the engagement of your customers, and you know that survey answers can help to predict retention. What do you do with all this information? Use it to build out a content marketing plan.

To do this, use a timeline approach. On the left is your

starting point, where you are today. On the right is a point that is a couple months after the customer has made their decision to either continue or stop receiving your company's products or services.

Now plot future events on the timeline. Start with the key meetings that will take place. For example, will there be a formal pitch meeting? Will there be an account review meeting during which you receive feedback on how your company is doing?

After that, think about all the different content you can put on that timeline. It's also a good idea to ask the client what would be most helpful. Think about what the customer's company is currently going through. What type of information do the company's leaders and others who influence buying decisions need to help solve their problems?

When the timeline is full, you'll have a big-picture view of the content that must be created for you to carry out the plan. Hopefully, some of the content will already exist. But if not, you'll need to consider the best way to create this content. We'll get into that in Chapter 24, "Different Ways to Create Content."

As you consider the content you will need, don't fall into the trap of publishing "one-way" content. What can you say, and in what format can you say it, so that your content engages your customer and demonstrates that you've listened to them? For example, sending out a survey is a great way to raise customer engagement.

Step 5. Monitor engagement and optimize the plan.

Great content marketers know that they aren't done after the content has been published; they know that the fun really starts when they get a look at what happened after publication. Does it look as if the content was interesting enough? How much time did recipients spend looking at it? Did they forward it to others in their company, or did they not even open the email? These are the things you need to monitor.

If a customer isn't engaging the way you thought he or she would, go back to the plan and timeline you built and think about other ways to connect with the customer. Do you need to change the topics the content covers? Do you need to reword the email? Do you need to change the content's format or channel? Should you provide the customer printouts of what you send via digital channels, to make sure they have seen it? These are all things to explore along the way.

CHAPTER 17

How Do I Change the Perceptions of Others?

A man holding an empty coffee cup stood outside a coffee shop. He made eye contact and smiled at each person who came out of the shop. It was a cold day right before Christmas, and the Salvation Army bells were ringing.

A woman emerged from the coffee shop and deposited some change in the man's cup and gave him a cheery "Happy holidays!" Taken aback, the man responded, "Hey, why did you just put change in my cup?" Which left the woman wondering why the homeless man was upset.

Well, he wasn't actually homeless. He was my father-in-law, and he was waiting for his wife to come out of the coffee shop.

This is an example of the power of perception. Making some assumptions, the generous woman expressed the holiday spirit by giving change to an idle man holding an empty cup. Her assumptions led her to a logical but incorrect conclusion.

Why is it important to share this story? It shows the speed at which one's brain perceives a situation—and how it can easily get it wrong. Because it doesn't have all the relevant information or the time to analyze it, the brain makes a series of assumption-sto reach a conclusion. Sometimes, it's accurate. Other times, it's way off.

Think about how many assumptions you have already made today. Now think about how many of them were incorrect. It's hard to even estimate how many you've made, much less how many were correct, right? That's because your brain quickly processed information, formed an opinion, and moved on.

The challenge for B2B companies is that, once a prospect or customer has formed an opinion about your company, how can it be undone? For example, your customer might not trust your company or think it doesn't offer the best products. He or she may think your team isn't agile enough, or your company is too expensive. Such obstacles can't be overcome overnight.

Content marketing can play a big role in changing perceptions. First, however, you must use research to be sure you understand how people are perceiving your company. There are a couple ways to do this.

The best way is to hire a third-party research company.

If you don't have the budget, though, you need to communicate directly with your customers. If you talk to them yourself, however, you're not going to always get an accurate read. Why not? Because of something called response bias.

Here's an example. Think about being at a restaurant where the chef asked how your meal was. When responding, you held back some information, probably because you didn't want to hurt the chef's feelings or feel awkward yourself, right? Nor did you want to spend three minutes explaining what was wrong with the pasta. Instead you smiled and said, "Everything was fine. Thanks for asking." The chef thanked you, and moved on, without receiving the feedback he or she actually wanted and couldn't improve without.

The same thing applies to market research. Prospects and clients often don't tell you everything that's on their minds.

That's why you receive more accurate feedback when you use a third party to ask the questions.

Keep in mind that accuracy doesn't depend on just who's asking the questions. It also depends on how the questions are asked. For example, if the chef had asked his customers, "What would you do to make the meal better?," the responses might have been more helpful. It's likely you would answer that question more thoughtfully, because it's harder to reply, "Nothing would have made this meal better."

The companies I've worked for held different opinions about research. Some couldn't get enough of it and fielded a survey every month. One CEO even sat in on the readouts. Other companies used their research budget to invest in something other than research. They didn't see the value of research and how it would help the company grow.

Larger companies usually have more resources for conducting research, which is a huge competitive advantage, because they can keep a finger on the pulse of perceptions of their companies. In addition, research on their competitors give companies a view of the total marketplace. For example: Why did competitor A's favorability rating move up 7 percent in the past three months? Was it because of a new marketing campaign, or did it launch a new type of sales program? Or perhaps those new print ads actually worked? These are the kinds of insights research can provide.

Learning from research about how prospects and customers think about your company can be very humbling. Factors never considered can surface, and perhaps the things you thought most important weren't even part of the survey respondents' considerations. Maybe you were sure that customers were unhappy with customer service, but actually it was your website's functionality that was frustrating them.

Once you have a good understanding of the negative perceptions of your audience, think about how to change them. What would your customers and prospects need to see or hear to change their minds? How can you convince them their perceptions are wrong? Can you do it quickly, or will it require months, even years?

It's also important to put aside ego and consider the possibility that customers' perceptions are accurate. Maybe you don't have a perception problem at all but rather a reality problem. If so, the problem is too big for content marketing to fix, and the company must have the courage to embrace the very real problem. Once a real problem has been fixed, then you can use content marketing to change perceptions of it.

Some people have the mistaken idea that content marketing can change customer perceptions without fixing the real problem. At one company, in response to the low innovation scores our perception research revealed, an executive said, "We should create a white paper and talk about how innovative we are. That will fix the problem."

I couldn't help but smirk in response. First, I realized that the scores were probably accurate, for the company had done nothing innovative of late. Second, even if the data weren't accurate, why would we use a white paper, a more traditional method of communicating, to be perceived as innovative? The solution was for the company to actually start doing things that were more innovative, and only then could we communicate that externally—and then only in innovative ways.

Even though each company has unique challenges related to its external perceptions, there's a common framework for helping to change them. Here are four steps you can take to overcome negative perceptions of your company.

Step 1. Measure baseline perception.

First, use research to establish a baseline. It grounds decisions in what your customers and prospects really think about your company. You can field the research once or twice a year. Ask a wide range of questions relating to various parts of the business. The key here is to cast a wide net to capture many opinions about your company.

Once the baseline has been established, make sure to ask exactly the same core questions every time the research is later fielded, so that track short-term and long-term changes in customer perception can be tracked.

Step 2. Determine whether the problem is one of perception or reality.

This is the trickiest part. You're going to review a lot of data, and something is most likely going to appear off. For example, your company might have just launched a new product that you believe is better than the similar product of a competitor, but in response to questions about quality levels of various companies' products, your company's new product receives the lowest rating.

Is this just a perception problem—that is, the audience doesn't know what it's talking about? Or is your new product not actually better than the others, perhaps even the worst of them all? You need to get to the bottom of this. To do so, you could conduct follow-up research by having people actually test the different products.

If those tests showed customers and prospects liked your product and expressed surprise at how good it is, then, thankfully, the problem is just one of perception.

If that's not the case and your product isn't good, your company needs to address that problem by making the product better.

Don't be naive and think that marketing can fix a real issue. After the product is improved, you can retest it with customers and only then move on to using marketing to improve the perception of the product.

Step 3. Create content that illuminates the incorrect perception.

Now for the most exciting part, if you enjoy problem-solving. Once the baseline metrics have been established, and you're sure that the problem is one of perception, your job is to solve the problem of how to change people's perceptions.

I've always looked at this effort a bit like a game, its object being to make the right choices from among all the variables. Whether you want people to perceive your company as more innovative or better at problem-solving or more environmentally friendly, what's likely to be the most effective way to change their thinking? What does the content need to consist of? What would be the most persuasive story, and who should be telling it? Should you base the content in facts or focus on emotions? What format and channels should you use?

These decisions are important because you're likely not to-have a person's undivided attention for a leisurely ten to fifteen minutes to make your case. What formats lend themselves to starting to change someone's mind in thirty seconds or less? Start with short-form content—perhaps an animated video or infographic. It can link to longer-form content, but never assume that people will give you the benefit of the doubt and make it to the end of any of your content.

Every situation is unique. Sometimes you need to develop

rational content. For example, if you learn people perceive your company as too expensive, you should demonstrate that it is in fact not, perhaps by disclosing prices earlier in the content marketing timeline.

Other times, emotional or personal messages may be required. For example, if research reveals a problem with trust, you could use videos of happy customers explaining your company's impact on their business and how much they trust your company's employees and how much they enjoy working with them

Demonstrating that choosing your company's product or service could help customers personally—perhaps make them look good to their boss or simplify a portion of their work—can be particularly effective. In a 2013 survey, Google and CEB found that "B2B purchasers are almost 50% more likely to buy a product or service when they see personal value—'such as opportunity for career advancement or confidence and pride in their choice'—in their purchase decision." The research also showed B2B buyers are eight times "more likely to pay a premium for comparable products and services when personal value is present."[33]

Step 4. Conduct follow-up research.

After you've created and distributed the content addressing the perception issue, it's time to go back and see if it's had any impact on customer perception.

When asking the same research questions that you asked

[33]Sam Nathan and Karl Schmidt, "From Promotion to Emotion: Connecting B22B Customers to Brands," Think With Google, October 2013, https://www.thinkwithgoogle.com/marketing-resources/promotion-emotion-b2b/.

in step one, be sure to also ask respondents if they have seen the content. When the results are in, compare the survey results from the group that has seen the content and the group that hasn't. Even if the content is linked to your website, it's impossible to tell who has or has not seen it.

At this point, you're hoping that the group that saw the content had a more favorable perception rating than those who didn't. If not, your marketing didn't work. In that case, follow up with the same customers to understand why their perceptions didn't improve. Make sure to have this follow-up question already in your research for this group, so that you can capture their responses in the same session.

When content marketing has done its job, you can make a claim that goes something like this: "We know that our customers who read/see our customer-testimonial video are 23 percent more likely to have an improved perception of us than those who don't."

CHAPTER 18

How Do I Launch My Product or Service?

In 1906, after a small vessel entered a creek that separated Atlantic City from the rest of New Jersey, a newly constructed railroad bridge was put back in place so that normal rail traffic could resume. But the first eastbound train to cross the bridge, a three-car passenger train, derailed and plunged into the water below, killing fifty-three people.

Two days later, Ivy Lee, a public relations expert with the Pennsylvania Railroad, issued a statement to the press about the accident, which the *New York Times* printed word for word. Thus the first press release was born.

This is the first documented example of a company successfully using a press release to communicate a point of view to a mass audience. Eventually, the technique of using the media to reach customers was adopted by companies with goals other than damage control. For example, they used press releases to turn their product announcements into news stories.

For decades, B2B companies relied on press releases to launch products. They notified various media outlets and hoped the information could be considered newsworthy. Because every industry had its own trade publications, they were the principal way companies got their messages out.

The role of the press release has changed in the past twenty years. First, in 1996, Google started sharing its press releases with the public. Until then, releases normally had been reserved for journalists. With everyone having access to the same information, journalists then preferred to rely on them less. Second, as the cost of issuing press releases plummeted as the process became digital, the number issued skyrocketed, making it hard for any particular release to stand out. In 2013 alone, the largest press-release services—PR Newswire, Business Wire, and Marketwired—sent out roughly 642,000 press releases.[34]

What's the modern way to launch something that doesn't rely on a press release? Apple set the standard in 2005 by conducting a live event—essentially a presentation to a large gathering of carefully selected journalists, influencers, and customers. Since Apple announced the iPhone at Macworld Expo in 2007, the worldwide live-presentation format has worked wonders for Apple. About two million people tuned in to the webcast of Apple's live event for its iPhone 11.

Few, if any, other companies have Apple's resources and cachet and can only dream about attracting such crowds. The best alternative is to attach your product launch to an event where your customers will already be. For example, if you're in the consumer electronics business, you'll most likely launch at the annual Consumer Electronics Show in Las Vegas, attended by 182,0000 people and 4,400 companies with exhibits that fill the space of about fifty football fields. The people you're trying to reach are far more likely to be there than at your company's own event.

A successful product launch depends on more than when and where your company hosts an event. So much depends on

[34]Lou Hoffman, "The evolving distribution and role of press releases," *Ragan's PR Daily*, April 10, 2014, https://www.prdaily.com/the-evolving-distribution-and-role-of-press-releases/.

how the company tells its story. Most companies default to the typical story line: Here's the problem. Here's the solution. Buy our product.

Even though that's ultimately the message you want customers and prospects to take away, you can tell the story more creatively. The following are examples of two different approaches, one better than the other.

In 2015, Apple launched an upgraded iPhone camera that took better photos. Phil Schiller, Apple's senior vice president of worldwide marketing, started his presentation by showing what he described as a photograph taken with a high-end camera. The composition and lighting were beautiful. The colors were crisp. The background was blurred to draw more attention to the subject's face. Calling the photo the gold standard, he then said, "I'm going to bring up a picture that was taken with a very high-end camera . . . and so it will help us illustrate the feature we're trying to achieve." Bringing up a stunning picture of a man in sunglasses, he continued, "The quality of the background blur, that's what's called 'bokeh.' And the higher quality of the bokeh, usually the more advanced and higher quality of the lens and camera system. . . . It feels almost 3-D, like the person is popping off the screen. It's a beautiful photo. So our goal is to try to do something like this, using the two cameras in the iPhone 7 Plus."

After describing how the new camera feature works, Schiller paused and said, "Now I'm going to show you the first picture we've ever shown the world of a depth-of-field photo taken from an iPhone 7 Plus. Before I do, I have to come clean on something, because I wasn't entirely honest before. The picture I showed you before . . . was taken on an iPhone 7 Plus."

The audience suddenly realized it had been duped—but in a good way, one that brought a playful and optimistic energy to the room. Everyone was thinking, "Wow, the new camera takes pictures that are just as good as a professional camera." Mission accomplished. Contrast that approach with how Google announced a software feature at its 2018 I/O conference. CEO Sundar Pichai demonstrated a use case for how artificial intelligence (AI) and machine learning could make appointments. Pinchai said, "Let's say you want to ask Google to make your haircut appointment between ten and noon. What happens is the Google Assistant makes the call in the background for you. So what you're going to here is the Google assistant actually calling a real salon to schedule an appointment for you. Let's listen." He then played a recording of how it worked.

The software was impressive, but why not use a more dynamic, story-telling approach? Just as Apple's presenter did, all he needed to do was hold back some of the information and said, "Let's listen to a recording of a phone call you and I make every day. These calls are boring. They take time. You'd rather be doing ten other things." He could have gone on to describe the feature and then said, "Remember the recording I played at the beginning? Well, it wasn't actually a person making that call. It was our software." Far more dramatic and memorable, such a presentation would have had greater impact. What's the lesson here? Think about the best way to tell your story.

As press releases and live events have been used to get companies' product-launch messages out, content marketing can help you launch your product. Even though the specifics of each product launch are different, you can use the following seven-step overall framework to complement your company's launch.

Step 1. Develop a timeline.

The first thing to determine is how many weeks the entire product-launch campaign will require. Some product life cycles, such as those in the aerospace and automotive industries, can be as long as three years. The planning for most launches starts six to twelve months before the official launch day. Consider the events coming up in your industry. How can you attach your company and product or service to those events?

Start by having an honest conversation. How good is your product or service, and what is its financial upside in the marketplace? Based on the answer, classify the launch and prioritize it appropriately. Don't assume that every launch should be treated the same way and allotted the same amount of resources.

Also, should you launch the product or service nationally? Or is it better to test it in specific markets, or with a handful of customers? Don't make the common mistake of going too big too soon. The last thing you want is a product that fails because it didn't meet the expectations set by your marketing. The other benefit of starting small is that the product can be tweaked before it's rolled out to everyone.

Step 2. Select two or three clients to pilot your offering.

The most effective launches I've seen are ones that involve real clients. Having customers tell your company's story has real impact. The story is more believable coming from them than your company. Who would you trust more to tell you how great a product is: the company that produced it or the company that has actually used it?

Select a few existing clients who are likely to see great results to try out your product or service, and document their experience. What did they enjoy? What surprised them? What features did they love? Take a journalistic approach to capturing their experience.

Depending on your business, you can have some fun with the launch. For example, for website builder Squarespace's announcement of an updated platform, its content marketers created a humorous website called "Dreaming with Jeff," starring actor Jeff Bridges. The website opened to text reading, "At Squarespace, we believe that even the wildest ideas should come to life in a beautiful way." When it was featured in a Super Bowl ad, people flocked to the joke website. The company hoped that those who went for the comedy noticed that the website was really well done.

Step 3. Create content based on the pilot's results.

Now create various types of content that bring to life the results of the pilot. Shoot videos of the client interviews. Write case studies from each client's perspective. Show the actual results they experienced. You will be pleasantly surprised by how much content you capture by spending only one or two hours interviewing a client.

Then translate the content into multiple forms. Don't just create a one-minute video. Turn that into quotes to use in social media. Create an infographic that lists what clients love about the new product or service. Write a case study about each client in the pilot.

Step 4. Hold confidential meetings with existing customers.

Before the launch of your product or service is officially announced, meet with your customers. But this isn't a normal meeting, because it will include a bit of showmanship.

Three or four weeks before the meeting, tell your customers

you have a one-week window in which to schedule a confidential meeting. Tell them you can't talk about the meeting until that week. Tell them you're launching a new product and want them to be among the first to know. They will be intrigued. You ask them not to mention this to anyone else. You could even take this a step further and ask them to sign a nondisclosure agreement (NDA). Even with signed NDAs, this meeting is likely to leak to people in other companies—so don't reveal anything that would be a real problem if leaked.

Once the meeting has been scheduled, the customers will be anticipating it, their expectations growing until you reveal the new product at the meeting. Customers will remember that they had an opportunity to see something before it's officially available.

This technique can be powerful, but bear two considerations in mind: First, you need to be sure you're following SEC guidelines about insider information. If what you're doing has a material impact on a public company, then don't use this approach.

Second, and this is the tough part about this technique: don't use it every time. Reserve it for big launches. If you use this technique and your product disappoints the customers, you and your company will lose a ton of credibility. What's more, your customer won't be interested the next time you use this technique.

Step 5. Take the story on the road.

Not everyone has enough time or interest to drop what heor she is doing to attend your meeting. Part of an effective product launch is taking the story on the road. This isn't just about customer meetings. It's about connecting into other outlets who can tell your story for you.

Beyond using the traditional corporate marketing channels, think about how you can use the employees of your company for content marketing. For example, you can tap them for the fast-growing universe of podcasts. Did you know that in 2019, an estimated 51 million people in the United States will listen to a podcast? And 32 million will listen to one every month.

Have a subject-matter expert from your company be a guest on a relevant podcast. The focus of the podcast isn't going to be 100 percent on the product launch, but you can find a way to work that message into the overall interview. Podcasts are always looking to have interesting guests on their show. And as long as you can agree to the window of when the podcast will be released, this is another way to increase the chances of your success.

Another idea is to create a barter agreement with the two or three clients you put in the pilot. For example, have them distribute your launch information through their social media channels. Or do a joint press release. Setting up a couple of these agreements can be very beneficial as it's a way to get free, relevant exposure.

Step 6. Make the announcement.

This is what you've been gearing up for; all your efforts have led to the official announcement of your company's new product or service.

Create a specific event where the announcement is made. In the invitations for the event, play up how exclusive the event is. Feeling special to be invited will encourage people to attend.

Apple is famous for doing a great job at this. Its invitations are always mysterious and tease the product just enough to evoke curiosity. For example, the invitation to the launch of the MacBook Air read, "There's something in the Air." The invitation to Apple's iPad launch simply said, "Come see our latest creation."

What's the best place to hold your event? Not in a conference room, that's for sure. A special venue conveys to the audience the importance of the launch. Think about how to tie your venue into something related to your product. Launching new software for elementary school kids? Have the meeting in a school. Launching new manufacturing equipment? Have it at the factory where it's being produced.

Once the announcement has been made, you're not done. Use the event as an opportunity to capture more content. Ask people for initial reactions to the product. How might the new product benefit their company or make their lives easier? Capturing such information in real time will be required for an effective follow-up campaign.

Step 7. Conduct a follow-up campaign.

After the announcement is over, use the opportunity to maintain momentum. Take what you capture at the launch event to create content that you "drip" via social media or campaigns aimed specifically at those who attended the event.

If the product is ready for sale, the sales force needs to be in high gear. The buzz about the event can be used to secure follow-up meetings. If your company has made a good impression at the event, it's hard for a customer to refuse a follow-up meeting.

CHAPTER 19

How Do I Get More Referrals?

Everyone knows referral programs are an important way to expand a business. According to the Edelman Trust Barometer, 84 percent of B2B buyers start the buying process with a referral.[35]

Beyond getting new leads from a referral program, there are additional benefits. The leads tend to close more quickly, and at a higher rate. Why? Buying really boils down to trust. And if you're working with a prospect who was introduced through someone the prospect knows, you've already removed, or at least reduced, the trust hurdle.

Even though sales and marketing people agree that referrals are powerful, not every marketing department has a formal program. Having a formal program, however, almost always leads to a greater number of leads.

A word of caution on referral programs. They are ultimately a reflection of the overall value your company provides to its existing customers. If a company doesn't have a great product or service, it's not going to have much success at getting referrals. While this point is fairly obvious, it's important to reiterate.

---

[35]"The Rise of Social Selling," Sales Benchmark Index (SBI), August 14, 2013, https://salesbenchmarkindex.com/insights/the-rise-of-social-selling/.

Start with considering your referral program. It doesn't have to be as simple as, "If you do X, you'll get Y." In fact, in the B2B space, your program might not need to include an incentive at all. Some people make referrals just because you ask them to.

If there is an incentive, decide if your customer receives it for making the introduction or if the referral needs to buy your product or service before your customer receives it. Most programs require a transaction, but if getting a higher quantity of referrals is a high priority now, you may want to provide an incentive for just the introductions. For example, "If you provide us with five potential customers, we'll give you X."

If you're using a structured program that includes rewards, make sure that the incentive is enticing. Tesla has had some interesting referral programs over the years. The company originally offered customers $1,000 if a friend they referred ended up purchasing a car. Now the company offers a referring customer access to additional Tesla products, like their Powerwall Battery. At one point, the company had a program in which the first person to refer twenty new customers in a region received a Tesla Model X or Model S. This is clearly more of a PR stunt than a real incentive program, but it was enticing. Who wouldn't want to be rewarded with a brand-new car?

Another example of a structured reward program is what I call the double referral: both the referring customer and the new customer receive an incentive. The idea behind this approach is that the referring customer feels good for taking care of his or her friend.

If you're convinced that having a customer referral program is important, we can focus on the steps to take to launch a program.

Step 1. Identify your best customers.

Not all customers are created equal, and you want to focus on your best customers. They already see the value in what your company does, which means they're more likely to be advocates.

When it comes to identifying the right customers, there are two schools of thought. The first is to start from a list of prospective customers and find out if any existing customers are connected to them. This is where a tool like LinkedIn comes in handy.

The other approach begins with your existing customers and describes for them your ideal customer. They already know your company and what it does, and they'll have a good idea of whether anyone in their network would benefit from working with you.

Step 2. Monitor how things are going.

After you've identified the customer, be smart about the timing. Is your company in the middle of an intense project for the customer? Are there nagging or unusual issues challenging the relationship between your company and that customer? If so, it is not the time to ask for a referral.

I've found that the best time to request a referral is when a customer is happy. Once I sense the client is happy with our work, I incorporate the request into a post-project survey.

Step 3. Give before you ask.

In his *New York Times* best-selling book called *Give to Get:*

A Senior Leader's Guide to Navigating Corporate Life, author Vishal Agarwal outlines a simple human principle that can be applied to asking for referrals. The general premise of the book is that you need to give something of value before you take something. What do I mean by giving? Well, it can be a small gesture like sharing an article about a topic you know your customer is interested in. Or it could be a more substantial gesture like taking a client out to a nice lunch or dinner. Whatever you do, the key is to give first. It's important to let the "give" sink in before you go in for the "take."[36]

Step 4. Ask.

Provide your customer with some context about expanding your business. Give examples of companies you are interested in working with. If you don't have people's names, give the customer an example of a buyer persona or avatar.

The means of communication are important. Never ask for a customer referral in email. Always do it in person or on the phone. Why is this important? The first challenge of getting a referral is having the person agree to help. You could say something like, "Would you be open to thinking about one or two customers who might benefit from working with me?" If you phrase it like this, it's really hard for your current customer to say no.

Step 5. Employ the warm introduction.

Sometimes when you ask for referrals your customer will

---

[36] Vishal Agarwal, *Give to Get: A Senior Leader's Guide to Navigating Corporate Life* (Jaico Publishing House, 2018).

agree to it right away, followed by something like, "Feel free to reach out directly and mention my name." This is the curse of a customer referral system. People rarely respond to such cold outreach, even when you use the customer's name.

Ask your customer to go the extra mile and make the introduction personally. To make it as easy as possible for your customer, offer to write a generic email he or she could edit and send to the prospect to make the introduction.

Step 6. Update and thank.

If the referred customer engages with you, circle back to the customer who made the introduction. Let him or her know how it went. Most important, thank your customer. A simple phone call, email, or thank-you card will go a long way.

Step 7. Give a gift.

What should you do when you've secured a new customer from a referral? Naturally, you want to send a special gift to the customer who helped you out. Or, if you're using a structured program, it's time to deliver on what you promised. For unstructured programs, it's really important to take the extra step and give a gift. This will encourage your customer to make additional referrals.

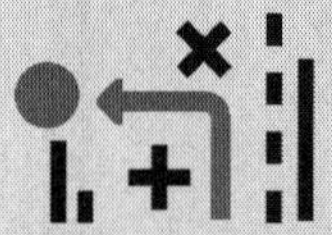

part V

CONTENT PLANNING

Planning out your content helps you avoid distractions and stay on track.

CHAPTER 20

Short-Term vs. Long-Term Communication Approaches

I've run five marathons and have hit "the wall" every time. The wall is the invisible barrier many runners run into near the end of a marathon. It hits me around mile twenty or twenty-two. My body says, "What are you doing to me? . . . Slow down!"

When you hit the wall, the body wants to stop, but eventually the mind takes over and provides the adrenaline rush required to cross the finish line. Sometimes, I get a minor leg cramp. Other times, the pain is more severe. One time, my calf muscle tightened up so much that I had to visit a medical tent. After a five-minute massage, I was back on the course.

What does marathon running have to do with content marketing? Both take the same sort of dedication. You don't just go out one day and run a marathon. You go through months of preparation. You follow a training program. You equip yourself with the right gear.

Continuing the running analogy, in content marketing there are two primary approaches companies take to publishing their content, a short-term and a long-term approach.

1. Short-term sequences (like a sprint)

The first, and less common, approach uses what I call sequences. This is when the marketer communicates with a specific customer with the goal of getting him or her from point A to B.

Sequence communications are shorter and require the marketer to demonstrate speed and nimbleness. A sequence might consist of communicating at all the touch points that are required to get a prospect to become a customer. Or a sequence could be a drip campaign that lasts for a certain amount of time and has the goal of onboarding a customer.

Sequences use a mix of inbound and outbound marketing. Even though the marketer wants everyone to get to the same endpoint, there's no single path for the customer to reach it. The content and timing change based on how the audience responds. Some audiences might take two weeks to get through an entire sequence; others never make it to the end.

The marketing team usually creates the content that enables the sales team to do its job. The sales team runs the actual sequence based on opportunities its members are developing. Fifty percent of the communication for a typical sequence can be based on templates, with the other half customized based on how the audience responds during the sequence.

If during a sequence you learn that a customer has a specific interest, you may want to either create a new article or use an existing one specifically for that customer. For example, the customer might receive an email like this: "Nancy . . . I remember that you said productivity is important to you. I've attached an article you'll be interested in. Let me know what you think."

The level of difficulty of managing sequences depends on

whether the right tools are in place. You need a CRM system to manage the touch points. The good news is that most CRMs have built-in automation tools, which make the whole process fairly straightforward and allow the salesperson to organize and track the effort more easily. (See Chapter 11, "How Do I Generate Leads?," for more about CRMs.)

The goals of a sequence of communications vary, but some goals that sequencing is commonly used to achieve are converting prospects into customers, onboarding customers effectively, raising the customer referral rate, and cross-selling products or services.

Here's the fun—or maybe not so fun—part, about sequences: their creation and refinement are never finished. Because your goal is to improve how each sequence converts, you test the variables—such as the channel, content, email subject lines, personalization, and frequency—by changing one at a time and seeing what happens. Rigorously testing and learning will help you land on a sequence of communications that performs better than others. And, once a sequence performs well, the conversion rate will grow a lot more quickly.

2. Long-term pulses (like a marathon)

The second publishing approach uses what I call pulses. Using pulses is more like a marathon than using sequences is, because there is a long-term commitment to publish content. This content isn't written and distributed to one person, as it is for a sequence. Instead, the content is sent to many people at the same time.

Brand, marketing, or communication departments are typically responsible for these long-term programs. They usually make a commitment to publish content on a regular basis, often once a week or every other week. More mature programs may be more intense, publishing up to four or five times a week.

Ongoing pulses aren't designed to get the audience from point A to B. Their goal is to create top-of-mind awareness among the recipients. Pulses are typically sent from platforms that reach many people, and articles and email newsletters are commonly the types of content they use.

A good example of such a program is the Marketing Solutions blog that LinkedIn has been publishing for several years. In addition to using this platform to publish the individual perspectives of its employees, LinkedIn also uses it to publish the work of several outside contributing editors.

I've been one of those contributors for a while, and it's a win for both parties. I get access to the LinkedIn audience, and LinkedIn gets free content that keeps its content-marketing machine going.

Sean Callahan, the senior manager in charge of the program, told me, "Frequency is important. You need to stay in touch with your audience." Publishing content regularly and frequently has led to some impressive results for LinkedIn.

Why do so many more companies use the pulse approach than the sequence approach? The biggest reason is that they want to stay in front of their customers. After all, the worst thing that can happen to a company is not to have a seat at the table. Creating, expanding, and maintaining its own platform, and constantly sending pulses of content to its audience, is a great way for a company to increase its likelihood of having that seat. And once a company has built up its audience, no media cost is involved, because the company owns the audience.

While the pulse and sequence are the two most common

approaches, some companies choose to take other approaches to publishing content. For example, when the time of year determines how people interact with or buy from a company, the company might publish content using a seasonal approach.

Whatever approach your company takes, you need to know how to determine what the content will be about and how to shape it.

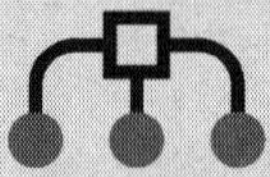

CHAPTER 21

Narrative Structures

Netflix will soon air a new show, "The Tale of the Murderous Wife." A man, obsessed with having a baby boy, tells his pregnant wife that if she gives birth to a girl, the baby will be killed. When she gives birth to a girl, the mother convinces an impoverished friend to raise the daughter in ignorance of her origins. Eventually, after many complications, the daughter learns her true identity, right before she is to be married.

OK, I confess: This story isn't coming to Netflix anytime soon. "The Tale of the Murderous Wife" is actually two thousand years old and from *The Golden Ass*, a book of stories that have endured since Apuleius wrote them at the height of the Roman Empire.

Why bring up "The Tale of the Murderous Wife"? To emphasize storytelling is far from new. Aristotle, born in 384 B.C., said that a good story must include plot, character, theme, diction, melody, decor, and spectacle.[37] He also said that a story must have three elements to be effective: pity, fear, and catharsis.

[37]John Geddes, "Aristotle on Storytelling in User Experience," Interaction Design Foundation, 2016, https://www.interaction-design.org/literature/article/aristotle-on-storytelling-in-user-experience; see also https://www.presspage.com/news/lessons-from-ancient-greece-aristotle-on-storytelling/.

Our world is filled with stories—not just to entertain but also to explain, persuade, and help build connections among people. Companies use stories to communicate with employees and stockholders as well as customers and prospects.

In his book Onward: *How Starbucks Fought for Its Life without Losing Its Soul,* Starbucks founder Howard Schultz discussed how a narrative was critical to turning his company around. He called a Starbucks store "the third place"—where one goes in the morning between home and work. Reinforcing this message helped create habitual behavior that has served the company well. There are about thirty thousand locations worldwide, and the company's revenue in 2018 was more than $24 billion.[38]

Let's look at another example. Remember the IBM campaign "Think"? That was in the 1980s, right? Wrong. It started in 1911, with company founder Thomas Watson. At a sales meeting, a frustrated Watson said, "The trouble with every one of us is that we don't think enough. We don't get paid for working with our feet—we get paid for working with our heads." To emphasize the point, he then wrote "think" on the easel at the front of the room.

Over the years, IBM has used "think" in various ways. It's been at the heart of many advertising campaigns. It was used to name the ThinkPad in 1992. In 2018, IBM's annual conference was called Think.

In fact, Apple's slogan "Think Different," introduced in 1997, was a subtle poke at IBM, to play up the differences between the two companies. Before the iconic slogan was officially introduced, Steve Jobs used a story at MacWorld in 1997 to illustrate the slogan: "You had to think differently when a first

---

[38]Howard Schultz with Joanne Gordon, *Onward: How Starbucks Fought for Its Life without Losing Its Soul*

computer arrived at a school where there had never been one before, and it was an Apple II. I think you had to really think differently when you bought a Mac. It was a totally different computer, worked in a totally different way, used a totally different part of your brain. And it opened up a computer world for a lot of people who thought differently. . . . And I think you still have to think differently to buy an Apple computer."[39]

Companies have tapped in to the long history of storytelling and narratives to communicate more powerfully what they stand for. Let's look at several different frameworks you can use for creating narrative content.

1. The hero's journey.

The hero departs the familiar world for an adventure, faces a crisis and wins a victory, and then returns home changed by the experience. This classic story structure, the hero's journey, has been used for thousands of years. The hero's journey was first studied in 1871 by Edward Burnett Tylor, the founder of cultural anthropology, who identified it as a story template for great myths and folklore of cultures all over the world. It was popularized by Joseph Campbell in his 1949 book The Hero with a Thousand Faces, in which he described the hero's journey this way: "A hero ventures forth from the world of common day into a region of supernatural wonder: fabulous forces are there encountered and a decisive victory is won: the hero comes back from this mysterious adventure with the power to bestow boons on his fellow man."[40]

(Rodale, 2011).

[39]Transcript of Macworld Expo, Boston, August 6, 1997, Mac History, https://www.mac-history.net/apple-history-tv/2008-07-19/macworld-boston-1997-steve-jobs-returns-bill-gates-appeares-on-screen.

[40]Joseph Campbell, *The Hero with a Thousand Faces,* (Princeton University Press, 1949), 23.

Campbell subdivided the hero's journey into seventeen stages, which can be organized in multiple ways and need not all be included in every story. Campbell broadly grouped the stages into three essential categories: departure, initiation, and return. These are the seventeen stages of the hero's journey, according to Campbell:

I. Departure

1. The call to adventure
2. Refusal of the call
3. Supernatural aid
4. Crossing the threshold
5. Belly of the whale

II. Initiation

1. The road of trials
2. The meeting with the goddess
3. Woman as temptress
4. Atonement with the father
5. Apotheosis
6. The ultimate boon

III. Return

1. Refusal of the return
2. The magic flight
3. Rescue from without
4. The crossing of the return threshold
5. Master of two worlds
6. Freedom to live

It's no coincidence that *Star Wars* follows Campbell's seventeen stages so closely. In 1975, George Lucas rediscovered Campbell's book, which provided the structure Lucas needed to finish the *Star Wars* script. After the movie's release, in 1977, Campbell and Lucas became friends. Lucas jokingly referred to Campbell as "my Yoda."

2. The hero's journey, modernized.

Hollywood executive Christopher Vogler is the one who coined the term "hero's journey," even though it had been studied well before his time. In the 1970s, he used Campbell's work to create a seven-page company memo for screenwriters called "A Practical Guide to *The Hero with a Thousand Faces.*" Vogler turned his memo into a book, *The Writer's Journey: Mythic Structure for Storytellers and Screenwriters,* in 1992.

Vogler said that "stories are devices that we use to raise awareness of ourselves about other people and our relationship to the world." He went on to say, "They can open up a door to a new way of understanding things or ourselves."[41] His twelve-stage framework, condensed from Campbell's seventeen stages, allows us to consider important questions like: Who are we? What's our responsibility? How do we deal with change in the world around us?

Here's what Vogler's hero's-journey framework looks like:

I. Departure

1. Ordinary world
2. Call to adventure
3. Refusal of the call
4. Meeting with the mentor
5. Crossing the first threshold

II. Initiation

1. Tests, allies and enemies
2. Approach to the inmost cave
3. The ordeal
4. Reward

---

[41] Christopher Vogler, *The Writer's Journey: Mythic Structure for Storytellers and Screenwriters,* third edition. (Michael Wiese Productions, 2007).

III. Return

1. The road back
2. The resurrection
3. Return with the elixir

Even though Vogler puts forth a clear order, he doesn't believe you need to follow all the steps perfectly and in sequence. He actually encourages storytellers not to, because sometimes altering one of the steps is enough to create tension and make the story unique.

3. Freytag's Pyramid.

Nineteenth-century German novelist and playwright Gustav Freytag analyzed the stories of Greek storytellers and Shakespeare and found that many of the stories used a similar structure.

He defined a five-act dramatic structure, which is called Freytag's pyramid, and is well known in the theater world:

1. Exposition: This sets the scene and provides the background information the audience needs to know about the characters and their challenges.
2. Inciting incident: This is a major event in the story that compels the main character to take some type of action
3. Climax (the apex of the pyramid): This is when the tension or conflict established in the first two steps is at its greatest.
4. Resolution: The problem or conflict is solved. You may think the story is over, but often there's more to it. Sometimes a twist appears to reveal something new about the characters.
5. Dénouement: The loose ends are tied up and the main character, or characters, returns to a somewhat normal life.

What's nice about Freytag's model is that it's simple. The visual nature of a pyramid to structure a story is crystal clear.[42]

4. The Golden Circle.

Perhaps you've seen the video of Simon Sinek's TEDxPuget Sound talk in 2009, "How Great Leaders Inspire Action," in which he shared a simple framework for marketers to communicate effectively. In summary, Sinek said, "People don't buy what you do; they buy why you do it. And what you do simply proves what you believe."[43]

In the talk, Sinek outlines his framework, called the Golden Circle. It consists of three concentric circles that represent the three parts of the framework—Why, How, and What:

1. The innermost circle is Why. Why does a company exist? Sinek says this is where every company needs to start thinking about messaging and storytelling. It's not about what you do, it's about why you do it.
2. The next circle is How. How do you do what you do? This tells the story of how a company differs from the competition. This is also called a unique selling proposition.
3. The outermost circle is What. The last thing to talk about is what you do. What industry are you in? What do you sell?[44]

Naturally, most companies start with "what," since it's easier to talk about what they do. Of course, you can't create a "why" without a "what," so you actually need to know what you

---

[42] For some applications of Freytag's structure to some famous dramas, see Rebecca Ray, " The Five Act Play (Dramatic Structure)," Storyboard That.
[43] Simon Sinek "How Great Leaders Inspire Action," TEDxPuget Sound, 2009, https://www.ted.com/talks/simon_sinek_how_great_leaders_inspire_action.
[44] Ibid.

do before being able to create your "why."[45]

Starting with Why is a reminder of the importance of making sure you create an emotional connection with your audience first. You need to earn the right to talk about your product and services, because people are not going to care immediately.

The strength of Sinek's Golden Circle is that when you first read about it, it really hits you over the head like a ton of bricks. Great brands use it all the time, for good reason. The shortcoming is that the communication model isn't really a story-telling framework. In my experience, it's useful to incorporate the Golden Circle into some of the other frameworks discussed here.

5. The V Formula.

Even without star power behind it, Dave Lieber's V formula is still worth sharing. Dave Lieber is a columnist for the *Dallas Morning* News. He has used a simple formula to tell unique stories twice a week for the past thirty-eight years. That's 104 stories a year! Here's his framework for writing his column twice a week:

1. Meet the character.
2. Hero gets knocked down by a villain.
3. The hero uses special powers to overcome the villain.
4. Dénouement. (The loose ends of the story are tied up.)

According to Lieber, the usefulness of his framework isn't limited to writing columns. "It works in a memo, a paragraph, a

[45]Simon Sinek, *Start with Why:* How Great Leaders Inspire Everyone to Take Action (Portfolio, 2009). Also see Sangram Vajre, "Simon Sinek's Golden Circle Explained for Marketing and Sales," *Inc.*, April 30, 2017, https://www.inc.com/sangram-vajre/how-to-use-simon-sineks-golden-circle-for-marketing-and-sales.html.

page, or a speech," he said. "Take the data of your life, and turn it in to real people doing real things, and you will move mountains. You will change the world."

6. The Story Spine (a.k.a. The Pixar Formula)

How has Pixar Animation Studios created so many blockbusters, like *Toy Story, Wall-E,* and *Monsters, Inc.?* Is it the company's amazing animation technology? Great distribution connections? Celebrity voice-overs?

Of course, all of these elements factor into Pixar's success. But did you know the company also has a story-telling formula that's used in most of its movies? It's called the Story Spine, an eight-line structure created by playwright Kenn Adams, the author of *How to Improvise a Full-Length Play: The Art of Spontaneous Theater,* in 1991 as an improvisation tool and for teaching storytelling and creative writing to kids.

The Story Spine formula is simple:

- Once upon a time _____.
- Every day, _____.
- But, one day, _____.
- Because of that, _____.
- Because of that, _____.
- Because of that, _____.
- Until finally _____.
- And, ever since then _____.

Adams called the Story Spine "a practice technique for learning how to tell a well-constructed story as well as an outlining tool to help construct a story."[46]

[46]Kenn Adams, "Back to the Story Spine," Aerogramme Writers' Studio blog, June 5, 2013, https://www.aerogrammestudio.com/2013/06/05/back-to-the-story-spine/.

7. The six-stage plot structure.

Another Hollywood storyteller worth mentioning is Michael Hauge. He's a consultant, lecturer, and author who works with writers on their novels and movies and TV scripts. He's on the board of directors of the American Screenwriters Association and has worked on projects with Morgan Freeman, Will Smith, and Charlize Theron. Hauge has worked with virtually every studio to help them tell better stories.

Much like Vogler, Hauge has documented the various stages used for most stories. Here's what his story structure looks like:

1. Setup (fully in identity)
2. New situation (glimpses essence)
3. Progress (vacillates between identity and essence)
4. Complications and higher stakes (moves steadily into essence)
5. Final push (retreats to identity, then returns fully to essence)
6. Aftermath (transformed existence)[47]

Hauge emphasizes the power of empathy in storytelling. "It's not an audience's or a reader's job to feel something. That's simply something you have to elicit."

Hauge has acknowledged his structure is something he has observed more than created and other frameworks out there can also work. In fact, he has said everyone is looking at the same thing; they're just looking through different windows.[48]

---

[47] Story Master blog, copyright 2014 by Michael Hauge, https://www.storymastery.com/wp-content/uploads/2018/11/6-Stage-Plot-Structure-Chart-color_.pdf.

[48] Michael Hauge, "Story Structure: The 5 Key Turning Points of All Successful Screenplays," Story Mastery blog, September 22, 2014, https://www.storymastery.com/story/screenplay-structure-five-key-turning-points-successful-scripts/.

8. The StoryBrand Framework.

In his book *Building a StoryBrand: Clarify Your Message So Customers Will Listen.* Donald Miller has used many aspects of the Hero's Journey to construct a framework for how businesses should tell stories.

The StoryBrand structure is simple: A character with a problem meets a guide who understands the character's fear, and gives the character a plan that calls the character to action, which results in success or failure.

Let's break that down into the seven basic elements of a story:

1. A character
2. A problem
3. A guide
4. A plan
5. Action
6. Success [or]
7. Failure.[49]

According to Miller, by using these seven plot points as filters for your messaging, "You'll be amazed at how each of these plot points help you clarify your messaging to customers. When there is clarity, customers are compelled and pay attention."[50]

This emphasis on clarity helps to ensure that people understand what the business does. According to Miller, if a company doesn't have a clear and compelling message, people won't

---

[49] Donald Miller, "Your Brand Is Not the Hero: How Story Will Revolutionize Your Marketing," 2019, https://storybrand.com/downloads/intro-to-sb/Introduction-to-StoryBrand.pdf; and Donald Miller, *Building a StoryBrand: Clarify Your Message So Customers Will Listen* (HarperCollins Leadership, 2017).

[50] Donald Miller, "Your Brand Is Not the Hero: How Story Will Revolutionize Your Marketing," 6.

understand what it does. And if what a company does isn't 100 percent clear to people, they are unlikely to do business with the company.

Like many of the other frameworks discussed in this chapter, this one is grounded in the premise that the story shouldn't be about one's company. The customer doesn't care about the company; customers care about themselves. To make an audience care about your company, you need to tell a story that is about the audience. Once you have customers' attention via a strong story, then you have earned your seat at the table to talk about how you can help them.

◆ ◆ ◆

With the existence of all of these frameworks and formulas for telling stories, why aren't companies using them more often? How come only Hollywood and book publishers seem to live and die by them?

Here's the reason: Companies love talking about themselves. There's just something inside us that wants to position our company as the hero. While this desire is understandable, storytelling doesn't work that way. It's rare that a customer falls in love with a company that talks only about itself.

Sure, you could argue that some of the bigger brands do it. Apple, for example, loves talking about itself. They do it in cool and creative ways and spend a bunch of money, but ultimately Apple's success is the result of its products. If you set your company up as the hero of your story, the story is unlikely to resonate with customers. It will instead be perceived as a commercial. After all, most of the advertising and marketing from the 1950s to 1990 positioned a company as a hero. Although this was apparently effective at the time, with the dramatic shift in the media landscape, it no longer has the same effect. Put another way, we have become effective at tuning out traditional advertising and don't believe that the role of the modern company is to be a hero.

You are not the hero in your customer's story. As Sean Callahan from LinkedIn put it, "You're the sword that the customer uses."

I can't tell you which of the eight story-telling frameworks discussed in this chapter is right for the specific purposes of your company. Each framework has its strengths and weaknesses. Experiment with them to see which ones work best for you.

CHAPTER 22

Personas and Types of Buyers

Think about the last time you were in a group photo. Maybe it was a group at a wedding or just a bunch of friends who got together. What did you do the first time you looked at the picture? That's right, you looked for yourself. Only after finding yourself did you look at everyone else in the photo. And then, before looking away, you probably took another quick glance at yourself.

Why do I bring this up? People, and companies, are obsessed with themselves. It's just how we're wired. Clay Stelzer, a director at Salesforce, has been in the customer insights and innovation space for more than ten years and is now in charge of coaching leaders at Salesforce. He put it this way: "People don't need your company; they need their problem solved." He went on to say, "Your product or your company is just one way of solving their problem. It's not about you; it's about the customer."[51]

Stelzer is on to something here. Even though you have to talk about your product to make the sales, the conversation shouldn't start that way. Stelzer added, "There's so much noise

---

[51]Clay Stelzer, interviewed by author.

in the world. The last thing they need is to be inundated with product information."

How can you force yourself to make sure you're not initiating relationships with customers and prospects based on your company's agenda? How can you put yourself in the customers' shoes?

Personas help with sorting this out. They are grounded in the idea that great marketing isn't just about the product or service you're selling. It's also about what the customer is buying. What's on his mind? What is she going through at work? This is a point in marketing where it's so easy to make inaccurate assumptions and go down the wrong path.

For example, in 2012, JC Penney's new CEO, Ron Johnson, made some radical changes in how the company went to market. He not only changed the merchandise in the store, he also changed the store's approach to pricing. He wanted to create a more high-end retail experience for customers, and he didn't like the idea of providing customers with coupons. He felt it cheapened the brand. He thought it would be better to just lower the price of an item by $5 instead of marking it up by $5 and then allowing customers to use a $5 coupon.

Turns out his customers didn't agree. They enjoyed the idea of saving money by redeeming coupons. Coupon redemption gave them a sense of being savvy customers. In an interview with *Time*, Johnson described the situation: "I thought people were just tired of coupons and all this stuff. The reality is all of the couponing we did, there were a certain part of the customers that loved that. They gravitated to stores that competed that way. So our core customer, I think, was much more dependent [on] and enjoyed coupons more than I understood."[52] He held

[52] Brad Tutle, "The 5 Big Mistakes That Led to Ron Johnson's Ouster at JC Penney," *Time,* April 09, 2013, http://business.time.com/2013/04/09/the-5-big-mistakes-that-led-to-ron-johnsons-ouster-at-jc-penney/.

the CEO job for only seventeen months.

If Johnson had understood how his customers felt about coupons, he could have avoided making his mistake. This is where the creation of customer personas comes into play.

What are personas? According to content marketer Ardath Albee, a marketing persona is "a composite sketch of a key target market based on validated commonalities—not assumptions—that informs content strategy to drive productive buyer engagement (i.e., revenue)."[53] Personas help you uncover insights and guide what content you share and how you share it with your audience.

Personas include demographic information but also go beyond it. At a minimum, all personas must include answers to the following questions:

Who is our audience—what are its demographics?

- Title
- Age
- Geography
- Income

What are the fears and motivations of our audience?

- Career goals
- Appetite for risk

Personas must be built based on accurate information. The process for developing personas of the audience segments your content will target must be customized for your company's unique marketing challenges and opportunities.

There are many ways to gather information, but I find the

[53] Quoted in Jodi Harris, "Quick and Dirty Guide for Creating Actionable Content Marketing Personas," Content Marketing Institute, September 10, 2017, https://contentmarketinginstitute.com/2017/09/actionable-content-marketing-personas/.

easiest thing is to conduct primary research—in other words, to talk with your customers. This can be done by having informal conversations yourself or by hiring a research company to orchestrate the process of gathering customer information.

The advantage of having an external company do it for you is that it adds an element of objectivity. After all, sometimes a customer just tells you what you want to hear. Having a neutral third party minimizes any customer bias.

If you're unable to conduct primary research with your audience—say, your firm's partners don't want you talking directly to their clients and there's no budget for an external vendor—another way to go is to seek out secondary research. Sometimes other people have already been in your shoes. Why not walk in their footsteps and use information that's already available? Look for relevant research on the internet, from relevant industry associations and market research companies. Usually, you can access the information on the spot or after paying a small fee. Market research companies like Forrester and Gartner charge anywhere from $50 to $2,000 for most reports, which makes them affordable to most marketers.

Getting inside the mind of your customer isn't easy. The more ways you can immerse yourself, the better. Phil Clement, my colleague at Aon when he was the global CMO, makes a great point of understanding the customer. He told me this work is similar to anthropology: "I think immersion is a really important idea. You should be out there. You need to figure out what's going on. You can't do this from the office."

All of the best marketing work I've been involved with had one thing in common: we marketers became very close to the customers and understood how they thought. Marketing and selling aren't designed so you can work in a bubble. If you have a genuine curiosity and really want to learn and understand what your customers are thinking, ultimately the solution to your marketing problem will be better.

Moving on from how customers think to how they act, you will see patterns emerge when you become immersed in customer-experience work. The patterns relate to the roles customers play in the buying process. Generally, when an organization is making a purchasing decision, there are four different roles its employees play. When creating marketing personas, be sure you understand these roles.

1. The decision maker.

This is the person everyone wants to meet, because he or she ultimately decides whether to do business with a company. Every decision maker is different. Some delegate buying decisions to teams and want to hear only their final recommendations. Others are more hands on, playing an active role from the start of the decision-making process.

The project's budget usually determines who will make the decisions related to it. The greater the financial considerations, the higher level the decision maker will be.

Most of the time, the identity of the decision maker is obvious and straightforward. However, usually some degree of organizational politics is at play. For example, some people might lead you to believe they have more decision-making responsibilities than they actually do, because they either want to be perceived as having the authority or just want to feel important. As another example, sometimes a power struggle might be taking place in the organization, perhaps as multiple people vie for the same promotion. In that case, someone who is an influencer today might be the decision maker tomorrow.

2. The influencer

The influencer is usually the person who is most readily available during the buying process. He or she is in charge of organizing the approach and selection criteria for the company's decision. Although not the decision maker, the influencer is crucial to the process. All it takes is one conversation with their decision maker, and they can alter a decision.

There are likely to be multiple influencers on any given project. The same individual could even be an influencer for one project's decisions and a decision maker for another.

3. The gatekeeper

The role of a gatekeeper used to be pretty straightforward. Screen phone calls and make sure you don't give anyone access to the decision maker, unless the decision maker wants to hear from them. While the same principles apply today, it's not that simple. Why not?

Every decision maker has an email address or social media account. So it's easier to connect directly with them today. For example, if they're active on LinkedIn, what's preventing you from posting a comment to get their attention? I'm not talking about doing this in a spammy way. Do it in a helpful and productive way. I've seen this technique be very effective. Someone invests the time to spend two or three months nurturing a relationship along, and then they follow up with outreach for the first time. The decision maker engages because they know the person already.

So, you can argue that the role of the gatekeeper's job has been altered in the past ten years. But gatekeepers do exist, and you need to understand the dynamics. If you build an effective relationship, they can grant you access to the decision maker. Upset them, and you may never have a seat at the table.

4. The blocker

Similar to the gatekeeper is the blocker, though the blocker usually has more influence. Why? They may have evaluated similar companies in the past. Or perhaps they even worked with the previous company. Or maybe they were a former employee at the company. For whatever reason, they have inside knowledge of a company and people value what they have to say.

Sometimes the blocker may not even be working at the same company. A decision maker or influencer might make a phone call to a friend or former colleague for an opinion. And just like that, the blocker appears. Don't get me wrong, the blocker doesn't have bad intentions. They don't actually see themselves as a blocker. They're just sharing the perspective on what they know. It's clear these types of buyers are written from the perspective of the company trying to sell. If the company described the blocker, they might describe them as the "insider" or "the experienced" perspective.

The other thing to factor in when trying to understand buying behavior is the number of people who work together to make a decision. Global services firm CEB did some fascinating research on buying behavior in 2013. By analyzing purchase timing by the size of the group determining the purchase, CEB found that the likelihood of a near-term purchase drops dramatically as the buying team gets larger.

Survey respondents were asked if they agreed with the following statement: "We will definitely buy from this supplier in the next six months." Here's how they responded, according to the size of the buying team:[54]

Number of people on team	Likelihood of purchase
1	81 percent
2	55 percent
3	60 percent
4	60 percent
5	53 percent
6-plus	31 percent

[54]"CEB Highlight Series: The Changing Business Customer," 2014, http://www.joshbarnes.net/blog/wp-content/uploads/2015/12/IconoIQ_395222.pdf.

part VI

CONTENT EXECUTION

When it comes to creating and distributing content, the content marketer has multiple options to choose from.

CHAPTER 23

Content Types

Now we're nearing the end of the planning process. We've reviewed how we're going to communicate—through an ongoing timeline or via a specific customer journey. We've developed a narrative by using one of the models. And we know a lot about our audience, because we developed a persona. Now the question is: where is the content going to live?

Before we jump into types of content, it's important to distinguish between content types and distribution channels. A content type is the container, or shape, of where we put the content. A distribution channel is how that content is sent. For example, white papers, case studies, e-books, and videos are all types of content. Email, social media, websites and trade shows are all examples of distribution channels.

When channels are in control of the company, there's no media cost to use them. These are referred to as *owned media.* If your company hasn't built such a channel, you will need to spend money to build and reach your audience. This is called *paid media.* Lastly, there's *earned media.* This is what provides the incremental reach of your content based on how many people share it with people who are not in your owned or paid group. Earned media varies based on how good your content is and how easy you make it to share.

In this chapter, we don't go over every possible type of content; there are just too many. For example, a printed book is technically a content type, as is a documentary film. The cost in time and money of these content types preclude their use by most businesses, however.

1. White paper and research report.

A white paper and its close cousin, a research report, are common types of content used in B2B marketing. They are appropriate for presenting an academic perspective, which means being sure that what you provide doesn't feel like marketing or promotional material. Educational and informative, this content type is relatively long, ranging from six to twenty pages, and often more for research reports. The longer format means someone who reads the whole paper spends up to twenty minutes reading it, which can boost the metrics.

It's common to gate such content, which means requiring people to provide their contact information before they have access to the white paper or report. Companies can invest several months as well as substantial cash in the research, writing, editing, and design required to create a white paper, and even more if the end product is a paper based on original research such as an industry survey. The payoff comes when people are interested enough to be willing to share their business contact information. This is how most companies gather leads.

Besides attracting external audiences, white papers and research reports can fill internal purposes of larger companies or academic institutions. For example, several years ago, Northwestern University undertook a large project to align its many departments over many campuses underneath a global brand. How did the university go about communicating with its many faculty members, deans, and other administrators? A committee of the Northwestern Board of Trustees wrote a white paper to help articulate the new vision.

2. Blog post and article.

Blog posts and other types of articles are popular with marketers because they are extremely flexible content types. They allow words, images, and sound or video to be combined onto one page. They also enable companies to more easily reap the benefits of search engine optimization.

Developing an article for a blog or other outlet requires the writer to research a topic—which may include conducting interviews with subject-matter experts—create an outline, draft the piece, have the content edited and, lastly, proofread before it's published. Once an overall design has been established for a blog post or other article type, not a lot of additional design or production work is needed. Most web CRMs allow content to be published instantly.

Blog posts can be generically published for the reader from a brand. Recently, however, there has been a movement toward content coming to the reader from specific individuals, often with their own unique perspectives. There's something about knowing that a blog post comes from a particular individual that makes it more credible. Publishing content from the individual also means companies can more easily scale their content, because every post need not be written by one writer. Although various writers will have different perspectives and will focus on different topics, it's important to have editorial standards in place for all blog content, to keep the reader's experience consistent.

Think beyond publishing content on only your own company's platform. It can be hard to build one individual's or company's own audience, and one way to expand it is to borrow someone else's audience. If the audience for a different platform likes the content, some of them will seek out other articles from the same source and follow the writer or company on social media.

Consider publishing articles in external publications. For example, SpencerStuart, a global recruiting and leadership development firm, published "The Leader's Guide to Corporate Culture" in *Harvard Business Review.* As a result, the firm reached a whole new audience via the business journal's readers, and it ended up with a published article to use for its own content marketing purposes.[55]

Also consider becoming a guest contributor on someone else's platform. LinkedIn's Marketing Solutions blog is one example of a platform with a lot of different contributors. Ever since it decided to publish contributing writers, the blog publishes content much more frequently, up to four to six pieces of new content a week. This is a win for both LinkedIn and the contributing writers.

3. E-book.

If you need to get the attention of someone you don't already have a relationship with, an e-book is a good way to do it. They're usually longer than an article, but shorter than a white paper or research report. They tend to be more casual and, oftenwith lists, tips, or checklists. Most important, e-books shouldn't focus on what a company has to offer. It should help the customer solve a problem.

[55]Boris Groysberg, Jeremiah Lee, Jesse Price, and J. Yo-Jud Cheng, "The Leader's Guide to Corporate Culture," Harvard Business Review, January–February 2018, https://www.spencerstuart.com/-/media/pdf%20files/research%20and%20insight%20pdfs/the-leaders-guide-to-corporate-culture.pdf.

E-books usually have more interesting designs and a variety of visual elements to capture the audience's attention. Because of this, creating an e-book requires a designer as well as a writer and is likely to take more time to create. Because people usually read e-books on desktop or laptop screen or a tablet, a design with pages that are 8.5 x 11 is fairly standard.

Make sure that at the end of your e-book you have a strong call to action. What do you want the audience to do? Be as clear as possible. This is usually the time to pitch your product/service. Make sure they know your company offers services related to your content.

4. Case study.

Case studies are great at telling the story of how a product or service has helped a customer. It's always more effective when someone else tells a story on your behalf, and in this case your audience will relate to the situation of the customer telling the story.

Put another way, "Don't take it from us, take it directly from our client." Using this content type to show social proof is very effective. A customer with big brand-name recognition makes your content even more credible.

A case study usually includes several sections: background or context, the challenges or challenges the customer faced, the solution your company provided, and the impact or results. Use the same organization for all your company's case studies so that your audience understands how you tell these types of stories.

Generally, case studies should be no more than one or two pages long, since they are brief snapshots of what has happened. The best case studies are based on interviews with the customers themselves and include direct quotations, which humanize the story and enhance the social proof.

Obviously, you need to get permission from the person or company featured in the case study. When interviewing your customer, try to get real numbers and specific results instead of generic descriptions. Sharing results in case studies is critical to making them believable as well as a more interesting read. If your client isn't comfortable sharing the raw numbers, offer to use percentage changes to communicate the impact without providing detailed data.

Case studies can live online as well as web pages or PDFs. Some companies choose to distribute printed-out color PDFs as well. Depending on the company, topic, and potential readers, sometimes spending more on the visual presentation and production values makes sense.

For example, commercial real estate company Jones Lang LaSalle used beautiful photography to illustrate "Every Building Has a Story," a leave-behind for prospective customers that showed what its design teams did to transform different types of spaces. The skillful presentation, supported by a website, captured the attention and imagination of their prospective customer, and the physical publication was an effective reminder of what the company had to offer.

5. Video

The popularity of video continues to grow. Videos are great at telling stories and capturing audience attention. It's also easy to watch a video, which requires less effort than reading.

Video was once very costly to produce. With more affordable equipment, however, today it's possible to create a cost-effective video. However, it's still a complex project to produce. You usually need three to five people to create it: someone to develop the vision, someone to shoot the video, someone to capture the sound, and then someone to edit what's been captured.

If you're lucky, you can find one or two people who have multiple skills. For example, the creative director can also shoot the video and perhaps even edit it. This approach can reduce both production costs and production time.

Live online video is a newer approach that is gaining traction. It started with companies like U-Stream and Meerkat. Today, virtually every social media platform has live-streaming. The appeal of live-streaming is that it's very efficient to make (since there's no editing). And, since there's only one take, what's being communicated is very authentic—which can make it more interesting to the audience. However, live-streaming can be stressful to create, since no editing means you can't go back and do anything over again.

6. Buying guide

A buying guide is a great type of content for prospects just starting to consider purchasing a category of goods or services. It helps them to understand how they should be thinking through and going about making their decision. The goal of a buying guide is to educate the customer in a neutral way. You want to describe how the entire category works and how a prospect should evaluate making a decision. You can even list out the pros and cons of each of your competitors, similar to how your customer would think about it.

The key here is to do so in an unbiased way. If you can do that, they're more likely to consider you. You want to get your customer to think like this: "This company really helped me understand how to think about this decision… I should include them as one of the companies I'm considering since they seem to know what they're talking about."

Buying guides can have design elements to them, although it doesn't need to be as splashy as an e-book. It's usually longer. It's not uncommon for a buying guide to be eight to twelve pages long.

7. Magazine

Publishing a magazine seems to be a dream come true for many B2B marketers. There's something enticing about a thick, printed magazine as the final product. I recommend magazines only if you are serious about making a long-term commitment. If you create a quarterly or monthly magazine, usually it's better to either build it in-house or work with an outside agency that specializes in magazines.

What's nice about the magazine approach is that a printed magazine is a physical piece. You can mail it to a customer or offer it in person. The obvious downside is the cost. Depending on how many you print, the cost might range anywhere from $1 to $5 per piece.

When you choose a magazine as your content type, don't expect to see a short-term return on investment. What's the best way to measure it? Customer research tends to be an effective measurement tool. You can ask your customers things like the following:

- Do you have a more favorable impression of our company after reading the magazine?

- How would you describe our brand after reading the magazine?

Magazines tend to be chosen by larger companies, with bigger and more stable budgets. Even at larger companies, it's not uncommon for a magazine to be printed for only two or three years. Then there's an initiative to reduce company costs, and inevitably someone says, "Do we really need to print this thing? Can't we just distribute it online?" The answer, of course, is, "Sure, we can create content and distribute it online. But that diminishes how its purpose is filled, because the physical copy of the magazine is what makes it interesting." So, again, if you want to publish a magazine, be sure there's a long-term commitment to do so.

8. Interactive content and tools

Most of the content types discussed in this chapter are examples of one-way communication; you're essentially talking at your audience. With interactive content, the audience role is more active. Examples of interactive pieces are quizzes, assessments, calculators, and games.

These two-way experiences are powerful for you and your audience. Beyond just capturing your audience's attention, you are finding out what's important to them. If you execute this content type the right way, this information is used to determine the messages you send in the future—or perhaps even remove from the mailing list the prospects who are not a good fit.

One of the leading companies in interactive content is Outgrow. Its platform allows companies to easily create and distribute interactive content. You can spend as little as five to ten hours creating a piece of interactive content within the platform before being ready to launch it. Plus, no coding is involved, so it's easy to use.

SEO companies use the tool approach all the time. They ask you to enter your website address and they evaluate how effectively your website works. This approach is useful to the marketer, since they're not just telling you how great they are, they're showing you what your weaknesses are. It's rare for a company to be able to show value this quickly and directly. And a real person isn't doing the work behind the scenes of an SEO company; with its tools, it happens automatically.

An early pioneer in interactive tools as free content is HubSpot. The company created a tool called Website Grader, launched it in 2006, and has graded more than four million websites since. After you provide your website URL, the tool, now called Marketing Grader, breaks out technical performance for a variety of categories, such as page speed, mobile friendliness, and SEO. It is also a great tool for competitive research. I've done many competitive assessments that showed how other companies' websites were performing. Actual website-performance data for competitors is a useful window into those companies.

With Ceros, another interactive content platform, you can create experiential content that's embedded into any web page. Adding this dynamic content to a blog post is very effective. With the use of this platform, I've seen increases by more than 25 percent of engagement metrics such as the time on the website and the amount of content shared. This is not uncommon. As Ryan Brown, head of brand strategy at Ceros, told me, "When you reimagine something from static to experiential, the marketing metrics always perform better."[56]

---

[56] Ryan Brown, interview by author.

CHAPTER 24

Different Ways to Create Content

Usually, the hardest part of content marketing is creating the actual content. People starting out in content marketing often think the content will come naturally—but they soon realize just how tricky content creation is without experienced writers and designers.

In this chapter, we review five of the many ways to create content. As with any other marketing project, you'll need to consider the budget, how long-term the commitment is, how quickly you need the finished content, and how much time you can dedicate to it.

Option 1. Build an in-house team.

If you can make at least a two- to three-year commitment to content marketing, building an in-house team is the way to go. You can start with a team of three or four people who can execute both online and offline work. You'll need a writer, a designer, and someone who can monitor and analyze the content's performance.

The ability to hand-pick team members is the main advantage of building an in-house team. Doing it will take some time, however. It's not uncommon for finding, interviewing, and onboarding employees to take two to three months. Among the additional advantages of an in-house team is that it's pretty cost effective if you have enough work for the whole team. Your costs are fixed each year, and you can create as much content as you can schedule for the team.

Through working together and using similar processes to create similar content over time, the team will also become very efficient and able to create content faster. In addition, a full-time in-house writer will eventually develop expertise about your business's subject matter.

Naturally, building your own team has some disadvantages. It can be hard to find the right talent. Why? Many content creators are independent contractors because they enjoy the flexibility of working on multiple brands and being able to say no to a project or increasing their rates when busy. And if one of the content creators leaves, it can throw a wrench into everything for a couple months, until the person can be replaced.

In addition, building an in-house team requires spending a substantial sum upfront. You need to factor in expenses like office space, benefits, and training. Plus, if you want to expand the team over time, you'll need to factor in hiring someone to manage the work.

Option 2. Hire an agency.

Love-hate relationships between agencies and their clients are not uncommon. Some agencies are great partners. Others say anything to win the job and figure out later whether they can deliver. Some agencies focus too much on their own agendas, such as winning awards, which causes headaches for their clients.

However, hiring an agency is an excellent approach if you want to both scale up your content marketing quickly and tap into people who know how it should work. These benefits come at a premium, of course, since agencies have to make money to survive and grow. Clients are often frustrated by the high cost, but that comes with the territory. Most agencies will bill based on the hourly rates of their various team members. Some are open to considering fixed-bid pricing, but only when they are comfortable with the scope of what's being created.

In addition, agencies are not known for having lean teams. It's rare to find an agency of only two or three people. Midsize agencies usually staff an account with four to six people. As for large agencies, it's not uncommon to have six to twelve people on an account's team. Extra layers can slow down the content creation and increase its cost.

Of all the B2B content-creation models, using an agency is the most unpredictable for clients. The team assigned to an account often changes over time, because someone either left the agency or wanted to work on a different account. And it's not unheard of for agency leadership not to spend as much time on your account as they should, perhaps, because instead they are focusing on winning a new account or increasing their margin on a fixed-bid project, and only show up for client meetings.

When the relationship is scoped right and the people on the account are good, an agency can produce outstanding work. They usually excel at conceptual thinking, generating big ideas and creating campaigns rather than one-off deliverables. Upon hiring an agency, you can instantly leverage its process, people, and knowledge. It's relatively easy to find and hire an agency, although the scoping process can take some time.

If you need to create content quickly, could use an outside perspective, and are willing to pay a premium, working with any agency is an excellent option.

Option 3. Use a staffing firm to find freelancers.

I've used staffing firms before, when I worked inside Fortune 500 companies. They're a great model if you need quick access to specialized talent and don't want to invest time in finding the right team. Within twenty-four hours of our initial phone call, the firm's account representative had two or three candidates ready for me to interview over the phone. Most of the candidates could start working within a couple days.

The primary benefit of using a staffing firm is the avoidance of the red tape required to hire a company employee, which can take weeks or even months. No long-term decisions are required; if you need someone for a three- or four-week project, that's completely fine, as long as you have set with the firm upfront the expectations for the length of the project.

The main disadvantage of working with a staffing agency is that it can take up to 50 percent of the worker's total hourly billable rate. This raises the chance of the person you're working with being underpaid, based on his or her market rate. And, if underpaid, the person is less likely to want to have a long-term relationship with the staffing company, or with you.

But if you like the agency's persons, can't you work directly with him or her and pay the worker's own billable rate? Nope. Most staffing agencies have both clients and freelancers sign one-year nonsolicitation agreements that prevent them from working directly with each other. You can, however, choose to pay a one-time fee to "convert" a freelancer into your company's full-time employee. This is a fair approach, and going down this path would probably be a little less expensive than paying a recruiting fee.

Another disadvantage is that a staffing agency handles only the matchmaking and billing. It isn't around during the project and brings no thinking to the table, which can be frustrating.

You need to be comfortable with the staffing agency finding the right person for you, and that's it.

Option 4. Find and manage freelancers yourself.

Finding and managing freelancers yourself is an excellent option if you're connected to various types of freelancers. Before jumping in, however, you should have experience managing content creators or other creative professionals. You need to understand how the creative process works and the type of structure required to get the best work out of a person. Sometimes it means providing specific guidance. Other times, it's about defining a problem and letting the freelancer solve it creatively.

If you're able to find freelancers on your own, this is usually a cost-effective solution. You're not paying for an in-house team, and you're not paying the markup fee of an agency or staffing firm.

But, as with option one, the best part is you hand-pick your team. You know upfront who you will be working with, rather than being at the mercy of people who have been assigned to your account. The flexibility of being able to hire a freelancer only when one is needed is a benefit as well. For example, if you need someone to write one or two articles, you can hire a person just for that. You don't need to commit to paying someone for forty hours a week for three or four weeks.

The biggest challenge of working with freelancers is that their schedules change all the time. Sometimes, they're available when needed and everything works out perfectly. Other times they're booked solid and have no time to work with you. This is why it's good to have in your "stable" of freelancers multiple people who can perform similar tasks—and to plan ahead, so that you can book the freelancers you will need in at least three to five weeks.

Option 5. Use a content marketing platform.

Content-marketing platforms gained traction around 2015, when marketplaces like NewsCred, Contently, Skyword, and Upwork became a legitimate way to find content creators. They work similarly to staffing agencies, except that you go online to search for the workers you need instead of working with an account rep or salesperson. When you find someone you want to hire, you are charged a fee but it is nowhere as steep as a staffing agency's fee.

These platforms can be great when you have a specific need. For example, using an advanced search, in less than five minutes it's possible to find a writer who has twenty-plus years of experience, works with SaaS startups, and is an expert in enterprise network security. Once you find what you're working for, you can review their online work samples to confirm whether they would be a good fit.

Quick, easy access to talent is what makes content-marketing platforms so valuable. Some of them offer services beyond finding talent. For example, Contently has content-management software that helps with collaboration, governance, and performance tracking of content, which could be helpful for those just getting started with content marketing. Some platforms offer packages that include account-management services. This is a nice option for those at larger companies who don't want to manage a team of freelancers and don't mind paying extra for help with the heavy lifting.

Option 6. Use a content collective.

A relatively new approach, a content collective is a blend of the agency, staffing, and freelance models. The collective option uses an on-demand approach—that is, the client pays only when its content is being created. It's ideal for companies that need content marketing but can't invest a large sum in building a team or signing an agreement with an agency.

Collective approaches are good for clients that don't have large budgets and are looking for people with expertise. The client receives agency-like service, as someone at the collective manages all the client's freelancers. And transparency allows the client to know the team it's getting. Often the client can even hand-pick its content-creating freelancers.

The collective model is also efficient, able to kick off a project quickly. Some collectives have moved to a fixed-pricing model. At my content collective, 26 Characters, we created a menu of the more popular deliverable items and services that includes various pricing assumptions. It virtually eliminates the scoping process, which is appealing to companies that need to have content created quickly. On the downside, unless a client books a collective's team for months at a time, a collective won't have dedicated resources focused only on your business. They might also work across different cities, so in-person meetings with the client can't be guaranteed. And, because the team members usually don't work on-site, one can't enjoy the luxury of walking down the hall and seeing them every day.

As with all the content-creation options, the pros and cons of the collective model must be weighed. But, it's an excellent approach for those looking to create content and wanting to avoid building an in-house team or contracting with an expensive agency.

CHAPTER 25

Measuring the Impact

Measuring the impact of B2B content is tricky. There's no one-size-fits-all approach. Throughout the years, I've used several ways of measuring the impact. Thinking through the pros and cons of the following five options for a particular situation requires a thorough understanding of the pertinent company culture and sales structure.

Why is this important? If you use a method that isn't a good fit for your particular situation, the way you measure the impact of your content will be neither practical nor believable. When choosing from the five methods described in this chapter, consider how easy the implementation would be, what resources and infrastructure are available to you, and how quickly the results must be available. Choose a method your company can stick with, so that the current results can be compared with results from the past.

1. Media equivalency

Put simply, media equivalency is the cost you would have to pay to generate the same number of impressions. This approach can be quickly implemented because you don't need infrastructure or technical resources.

Here's an example of how it works. Let's say your content generated 800,000 impressions on LinkedIn last month. If you used a paid LinkedIn campaign to reach the same target, you would have been charged a cost per 1,000 impressions (CPM) of $14. Eight hundred thousand impressions were generated, which is the equivalent of $11,200 (800 x $14). This is also what's known as "earned media," the number of media impressions earned after your message reaches people online.

This type of model has been around for a while. It started when public relations departments wanted to quantify the value of media placements it received. For example, the appearance in the *New York Times* of your company's story or quote from an executive has a value. PR departments determined the value based on how much room the coverage took up in the paper and paper's circulation.

Not everyone believes in media equivalency. Some are skeptical because it's not a tangible thing. After all, the value generated doesn't end up as cash in a bank account. While there is something to be said for this approach being somewhat theoretical, I like that it uses market-rate CPMs to determine the value of what it would cost to distribute your message in a paid channel.

2. Lead generation

Most marketers measure the impact of their content by counting how many leads it enables them to capture. As touched on in Chapter 23, "Content Types," these leads are captured by gating content behind a required form. The user receives access to the content in exchange for providing his or her contact information. These leads are then handed over to the sales team, who nurture the leads until they become real customers.

The nice thing about this approach is that it measures the direct impact of content on revenue. You can clearly say that a gated article posted on your company website created ten leads, and that three of them converted into actual customers. Add up all the revenue from each of the three leads, and that's the amount of revenue generated by the content marketing effort.

Then look at how much that particular marketing effort (the article) cost relative to how much revenue it brought in. The result is the return on investment, or ROI, for that article. This is why lead generation is the most popular and noncontroversial way to measure the effectiveness of content marketing. It's hard to dispute, since it clearly identifies the number of generated leads per marketing effort.

Lead generation also allows your content marketing's effectiveness to improve over time. After creating various pieces of content, you'll know which ones work and can tweak the others to improve their performance. The lead generation results of individual pieces of content should affect your approach to creating content. You could make the case, for example, that company resources are better spent on videos than blogs, or that content organized as case studies are downloaded more than general articles. Clearly, a lot of variables, including topic, format, design, and quality of execution, go into the performance of a piece of content, but over time the lead generation results will give you a feel for what's working and what isn't.

For this approach to be effective, you need a way to capture the leads and pass them along to the sales team. You also need a sales team that follows up and lets you know how each of the leads has performed.

3. Market research

If you have the resources to conduct market research, it can be an effective tool to measure the long-term impact of your content. This approach uses customer research to measure how people feel about the content you create.

This is a pretty straightforward approach. You can use this as a one-off research initiative or tie it into your company's existing research. If you have a Net Promoter Score (NPS) program, as discussed in Chapter 16, "How Do I Improve Customer Retention?," this is an ideal question to slip into that survey.

You can ask a variety of questions to learn about what people think of your company. There are a variety of best practices for how to ask these questions, which we're not going into here. Just know that the way you ask the questions is really important. And you want to make the questions consistent over time, so that the results are comparable and you can monitor trends over time.

Market research is great because you collect information from your actual customers. The results are helpful for aligning internal teams on what to focus on. After all, it's hard to argue with an editorial direction when your customers are telling you that's what they want and need.

4. Sales force feedback

This is a down-and-dirty approach to seeing how content is working. It's not the best approach, because the feedback is not coming from your prospects or customers. But marketers can take what you learn from their sales teams as directional learning.

With this approach, you send a five- to ten-question survey to the sales team. Ask them if they think the B2B content you're creating is of any value. Make sure to frame the question in a way that focuses on the customer. For example, "What would your customers say about the content we create for them?"

The strength of this approach is that the cost is extremely low and implementation is easy. You can create a survey in ten minutes and have your head of sales send it out. You can also use this survey to generate new content ideas, since the sales force understands well what's happening in the marketplace.

A word of caution: what your sales team wants and what your customers want may be two different things. Sometimes customers don't reveal everything to a salesperson. And sometimes salespeople don't always ask the right questions to determine customer pain or needs. So, again, don't use this technique as the only way to understand how effective your content is.

5. Test and control groups

This is the most complex methodology for measuring content-marketing performance. When implemented, however, it can provide proof of the content's impact. You split the same audience into two groups, the test and the control groups, and test different variables to understand the incremental lift. Youneed the right tools to set up the tests, but these are standard these days and easy to use.

You can test something as simple as different subject lines or pieces of copy. For example, in testing a renewal direct-mail piece for a fitness company mailed in March, the line "Swimsuit season is right around the corner" drove a lift in overall conversion compared to the control group. It's amazing to see what one small tweak like that can have on performance.

Tests aren't always so simple. For example, I've tested the effects of a series of tactics in one group of cities and a different series of tactics in a similar group of cities. We then looked at the difference in the two groups' brand awareness and sales. The results helped us to determine the mix of marketing tactics and budgets that would optimize performance.

The main advantage of using test and control groups is that it's a data-driven approach that provides a conclusion. You can also perform a chi-squared test to understand how confident you are that you can replicate the test results. Companies that embrace test and control are usually better at making more sound decisions about their sales and marketing. Why? There's no guessing about the outcome; you're letting the numbers tell you how to move forward.

You know you're in a test-and-control culture when someone says something like, "Interesting idea . . . we should test it." Letting the data make the decisions also helps reduce internal resistance to adopting new ideas and approaches. Endless debates can be avoided by basing decisions on the numbers.

part VII

CONCLUSION

Now that you understand the value and techniques used in problem-solving, you need to remind yourself that there are some problems you can't see.

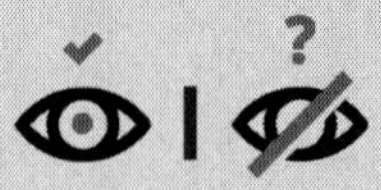

CHAPTER 26

Known vs. Unknown Problems

Outside CIA headquarters in Langley, Virginia, is a sculpture called Kryptos. Created by artist James Sanborn in 1990, it's twelve feet high and consists of four curved copper panels on which a total of 1,735 letters appear. The encrypted messages on three of the panels have been decoded.

According to the CIA website, "Mr. Sanborn worked for four months with a retired CIA cryptographer to devise the codes used in the sculpture." Only two people in the world know the message: Sanborn and Willian Webster, who headed the CIA when the art was commissioned. Webster insisted on learning the decoded messages to ensure it wouldn't embarrass the agency.

Several CIA and National Security Administration (NSA) employees have deciphered the first three panels, and CIA analyst and amateur cryptographer David Stein is one of them.

This is his description of breaking the code for first message:

> And suddenly it happened. I was hit by that sweetly ecstatic, rare experience that I have heard described as a "moment

of clarity." All the doubts and speculations about the thousands of possible alternate paths simply melted away, and I clearly saw the one correct course laid out in front of me. Taking a fresh sheet of paper, I slowly and deliberately wrote out a new column of letters, followed by another, and then another. . . . After more than seven years encompassing some 400 hours of laboring over piles of paper covered with gibberish, I was at last looking down at a paragraph of clear English text. I had broken out the first part of the Kryptos code.[57]

The cryptic message on the first panel is something Sanborn created:

> Between subtle shading and the absence of light lies the nuance of iqlusion.

The second message, also cryptic, refers to something that's buried. With a little punctuation added, it reads as follows:

> It was totally invisible. How is that possible? They used the Earth's magnetic field. The information was gathered and transmitted underground to an unknown location. Does Langley know about this? They should. It's buried out there somewhere. Who knows the exact location? Only WW. This was his last message. Thirty-eight degrees fifty-seven minutes six point five seconds north, seventy-seven degrees eight minutes forty-four seconds west ID by rows.

The third message is from Howard Carter's diary, his description of opening King Tut's tomb in 1922:

> Slowly, desperately slowly, the remains of passage debris that encumbered the lower part of the doorway was removed. With trembling hands I made a tiny breach in the upper left-hand corner, and then, widening the hole a

---

[57] David D. Stein, "The Puzzle at CIA Headquarters: Cracking the Courtyard Crypto," https://elonka.com/kryptos/mirrors/daw/steinarticle.html.

little, I inserted the candle and peered in. The hot air escaping from the chamber caused the flame to flicker, but presently details of the room within emerged from the mist. Can you see anything? The hot air escaping from the chamber caused the flame to flicker, but presently details of the room within emerged from the mist. Can you see anything?

Although Sanborn has revealed two words of the fourth message ("Berlin clock), the remaining eighty-six characters of the last panel remain a famous unsolved puzzle. Furthermore, even if someone deciphers the final message, the mystery isn't solved. Using the four decoded messages, someone would still need to solve the actual riddle of *Kryptos*.

Kryptos is an instance of the problem staring you in the face. The reality in the content marketer's day is exactly the opposite. Problems that we're not even aware of surround us. What we think is the problem might be a symptom of the problem; it's common for the real problem to lie below the surface, waiting to be discovered.

The ability to find and solve problems is critical in business and life. Surprisingly, most people are unaware of actual problem-solving techniques. During the interviews conducted for this book, I asked everyone the same question: "How do you solve problems?" With the exception of three people, everyone answered that they weren't sure. They followed no process. They used none of the problem-solving techniques described in this book.

The goal of this book is to help you understand the importance of finding the right problem. We identified several techniques and discussed some of the most common business problems. We then focused on solutions to problems in the form of content marketing.

We reviewed the planning phases of how to solve problems with content including when to share your content, different storytelling approaches, and how to make sure your messaging resonates with your audience. We also got into the mechanics of executing an actual content marketing program - choosing different content types, how to create and distribute content, and how to measure everything.

I wrote this book to help you understand the problems you're facing at work. Within a week of finishing this book, you're going to be presented with a situation. Your boss may bring you into a meeting. Or you may be talking to a customer who shares something that's been frustrating them. Or, you may be looking at a month end report that says you're not selling enough.

You may find a surface-level problem, and think that you've solved the problem. When this happens, slow down. Use some of the techniques in this book to think through what you're really up against.

Dig deeper to make sure you really understand what's going on. Ask questions. Talk to people. Be curious. Don't stop asking yourself "Why?" Most important, make sure that the answer to the following question is clear: What's your problem?

Selected Bibliography

Adams, Kenn. *How to Improvise a Full-Length Play: The Art of Spontaneous Theater.* Allworth Press, 2008.

Agarwal, Vishal. *Give to Get: A Senior Leader's Guide to Navigating Corporate Life.* Jaico Publishing House, 2018.

Bell, Chip R., and Ron Zemke. *Managing Knock Your Socks Off Service.* Amacom, 1989 (first edition), 2013 (third edition).

Campbell, Joseph. *The Hero with a Thousand Faces.* Princeton University Press, 1949 (first edition); New World Library, 2008 (third edition).

Campbell, Joseph, with Bill Moyers. *The Power of Myth.* Doubleday, 1988; Anchor, 1991.

Campbell, Joseph, director. *The Power of Myth.* 1988 six-season public television series available on DVD and streaming services.

Chronicle, Edward P., Thomas C. Ormerod, and James N. MacGregor. "When Insight Just Won't Come: The Failure of Visual Cues in the Nine-Dot Problem." *Quarterly Journal of Experimental Psychology,* Section A, 54(3) (August 1, 2001): 903–919. https://doi.org/10.1080/713755996.

Content Marketing Institute.
https://contentmarketinginstitute.com/.

Creative Education Foundation.
http://www.creativeeducationfoundation.org/.

Geddes, John. "Aristotle on Storytelling in User Experience." Interaction Design Foundation, 2016.

Harris, Jodi. "Quick and Dirty Guide for Creating Actionable Content Marketing Personas." Content Marketing Institute. September 10, 2017. https://contentmarketinginstitute.com/2017/09/actionable-content-marketing-personas/.

Hauge, Michael. Story Mastery blog.
https://www.storymastery.com/.

Hauge, Michael. *Storytelling Made Easy: Persuade and Transform Your Audiences, Buyers, and Clients—Simply, Quickly, and Profitably.* Indie Books International, 2017.

Hurson, Tim. *Think Better: An Innovator's Guide to Productive Thinking.* McGraw-Hill, 2007.

Hwang, Sooa. "Storytelling in Branding: The Difference in Brand Archetypes Between Western and Asian Tech Brands—Based on Carl Jung's 12 Archetypes Model." Aalto University School of Business, Helsinki, Finland, 2017.

Hyman, Mark, M.D. "The Doctor's Farmacy with Mark Hyman, M.D." Regular podcast

John Deere Company, *The Furrow,*
https://www.johndeerefurrow.com/.

Junger, Sebastian. *The Perfect Storm: A True Story of Men Against the Sea.* W. W. Norton, 1997.

Miller, Donald. *Building a StoryBrand: Clarify Your Message So Customers Will Listen.* HarperCollins Leadership, 2017.

Miller, Donald. "Your Brand Is Not the Hero: How Story Will Revolutionize Your Marketing," a PDF designed to accompany the "Introduction to StoryBrand" video;
https://storybrand.com/downloads/intro-to-sb/Introduction-to-StoryBrand.pdf, 2019.

Miller, Paddy, and Thomas Wedell-Wedellsborg. *Innovation As Usual: How to Help Your People Bring Great Ideas to Life.* Harvard Business Review Press, 2013.

Ohno, Taiichi. *Toyota Production System:* Beyond Large-Scale Production. Productivity Press, 1988.

Osborn, Alex. *Your Creative Power.* Scribner, 1948;
Read Books, 2008.

Press Page. "Lessons from Ancient Greece—Aristotle on Storytelling." https://www.presspage.com/news/lessons-from-ancient-greece-aristotle-on-storytelling/.

Schultz, Howard, with Joanne Gordon. *Onward: How Starbucks Fought for Its Life without Losing Its Soul.* Rodale Books, 2011.

Sinek, Simon. *Start with Why: How Great Leaders Inspire Everyone to Take Action.* Portfolio, 2009.

Stein, David D. "The Puzzle at CIA Headquarters: Cracking the Courtyard Crypto," circa 2002. https://elonka.com/kryptos/mirrors/daw/steinarticle.html.

Vogler, Christopher. *The Writer's Journey: Mythic Structure for Storytellers and Screenwriters,* third edition.
Michael Wiese Productions, 2007.

Voss, Chris, and Tahl Roz. *Never Split the Difference: Negotiating As If Your Life Depended On It.* Harper Business, 2016.

STEVE GOLDHABER

About the Author

Steve Goldhaber is one of a rare breed of marketers who is equally adept at, and equally passionate about, creativity and technology. In a digital age that has forever altered traditional marketing techniques, these dual skills give him an in-depth understanding of how technology can be used to execute more effective marketing programs.

In his work in a variety of corporate settings—from small startups to complex global organizations—Goldhaber has demonstrated an ability to break new ground, disrupt the status quo, and get results. His broad view of marketing in a digital world has been refined over nearly two decades in agency and corporate marketing positions in multiple industries.

In 2017, Goldhaber started 26 Characters, a B2B marketing company. Previously, Goldhaber was in charge of global digital marketing for two Fortune 500 companies, JLL and Aon, where he was responsible for web, social media, search, mobile, and content marketing. Prior to that, he spent nine years at Digitas, a global marketing and technology agency. As vice president, he led senior clients and internal teams in building marketing programs that embraced leading-edge tools to create better customer experiences.

With a bachelor's degree in communications from Purdue University, Goldhaber is a regular speaker at industry conferences and has won several digital and integrated-marketing awards. He has been a judge for the Effie awards and on the advisory board for Social Media Week. He's also a product adviser for LinkedIn, helping to shape the road map for future service enhancements. Goldhaber has also been a contributing writer for LinkedIn, the Content Marketing Institute, and B2B Marketing.

As easily as Goldhaber can discuss solving a complex marketing problem with imaginative strategy, he can recount the challenges of completing five marathons, two urban adventure races, and travel to more than fifty countries. His Twitter handle is @goldhaber.

Goldhaber lives in Oak Park, Illinois, with his wife, Carolyn, and sons Andrew and Charlie.

Answer to 9 dot problem

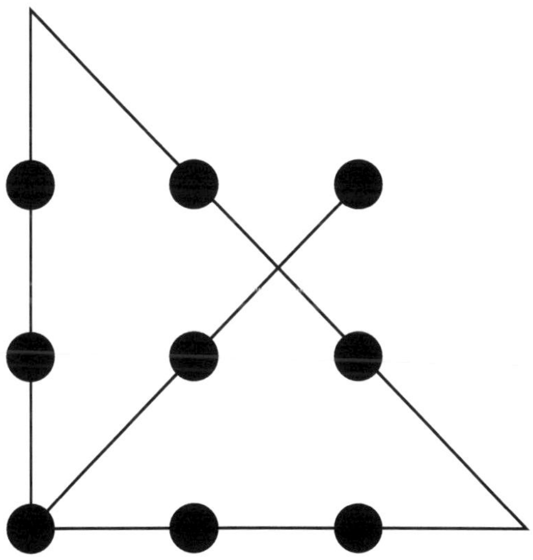

Printed in Great Britain
by Amazon

22624745R00155